T0316730

Cambridge Elements

Elements in Global Urban History
edited by
Michael Goebel
Graduate Institute Geneva
Tracy Neumann
Wayne State University
Joseph Ben Prestel
Freie Universität Berlin

AFRICA IN URBAN HISTORY

Ambe J. Njoh
University of South Florida

CAMBRIDGE
UNIVERSITY PRESS

Shaftesbury Road, Cambridge CB2 8EA, United Kingdom

One Liberty Plaza, 20th Floor, New York, NY 10006, USA

477 Williamstown Road, Port Melbourne, VIC 3207, Australia

314–321, 3rd Floor, Plot 3, Splendor Forum, Jasola District Centre, New Delhi – 110025, India

103 Penang Road, #05–06/07, Visioncrest Commercial, Singapore 238467

Cambridge University Press is part of Cambridge University Press & Assessment, a department of the University of Cambridge.

We share the University's mission to contribute to society through the pursuit of education, learning and research at the highest international levels of excellence.

www.cambridge.org
Information on this title: www.cambridge.org/9781009500722

DOI: 10.1017/9781009446839

First published 2024

A catalogue record for this publication is available from the British Library

ISBN 978-1-009-50072-2 Hardback
ISBN 978-1-009-44684-6 Paperback
ISSN 2632-3206 (online)
ISSN 2632-3192 (print)

Africa in Urban History

Elements in Global Urban History

DOI: 10.1017/9781009446839
First published online: December 2024

Ambe J. Njoh
University of South Florida

Author for correspondence: Ambe J. Njoh, njoh@usf.edu

Abstract: This Element in Global Urban History seeks to promote understanding of the urban history of Africa. It does so by undertaking four main tasks. Firstly, it employs race, ethnicity, class, and conflict theory as conceptual frameworks to analyze the spatial structures, social, and political-economic dynamics of African cities from global, comparative, and transnational perspectives. Secondly, it proposes a new typology of the continent's cities. Thirdly, it identifies and draws into focus an important but oft-ignored part of Africa's urban history, namely indigenous cities. It focuses more intensely on the few that still exist to date. Fourthly, it employs conflict, functional, and symbolic interactionist theories as well as elements of the race ideology to explain the articulation of racism, ethnicity and classism in the continent's urban space. This is done mainly, but not exclusively from historical perspectives.

Keywords: urbanization, urban history, urban sociology, urban geography, urban planning, governance

ISBNs: 9781009500722 (HB), 9781009446846 (PB), 9781009446839 (OC)
ISSNs: 2632-3206 (online), 2632-3192 (print)

Contents

1 Background and Foundational Matter

1.1 Introduction

Classical urban history literature contains only paltry information on the African urban experience. Some of the works are deafeningly silent on this subject. For example, no African city appears in the table of contents of Leonard Cottrell's (1957) *Lost Cities,* Robert Silverberg's (1962) *Lost Cities and Vanished Civilizations,* and Peter Hall's (1966) *The World Cities.* One of the few notable exceptions is James Morris's 1963 literary thumb sketch of (global) cities. It includes vivid journalistic accounts of seven African cities, namely Accra, Ghana; Addis Ababa, Ethiopia; Algiers, Algeria; Cairo, Egypt; Cape Town, and Johannesburg, South Africa; and Kano, Nigeria. Thus, one would be forgiven for erroneously believing that the history of Africa is devoid of urban experience. Hull (1976) noted this as a common misconception about Africa. Nevertheless, the misconception remains. As Hull once said, this fallacy holds that "Blacks did not build towns and that they lacked the political sophistication and organization to do so" (p. xiii).

The fallacy is afforded a life of its own by disparaging characterizations of the physical structure and architecture of the continent's human settlements. In one of her authoritative works on African traditional architecture, Labelle Prussin narrates a tale showing how this misconception is often popularized in the media. The tale is that of a team of photographers dispatched to Africa by a well-known American news magazine. The magazine was running a pictural story on world architecture and had assigned the photographers to capture pictures of African indigenous architecture for inclusion. After a sojourn in Africa, the photographers returned with no pictures and complained that the continent contained nothing of architectural value. In the words of the photographers, "all we could find were a bunch of mud huts" (Prussin, 1986: 183).

Nothing could be further from the truth! As I show throughout this Element, precolonial Africa contained monumental structures reflecting sophisticated architectural ingenuity. The massive palaces in the ancient capitals of Buganda and Bunyoro in East Africa, the Monarch's Obelisks at Aksum in contemporary Ethiopia, and the colossal walls that encircled the ancient City of Benin in present-day Nigeria and Great Zimbabwe are just a few examples. Although it had become fashionable for Western urban historians to feign ignorance of the accomplishments of ancient Africans in urban and architectural development, there is abundant evidence that they have always been aware of Africa's rich urban history. The fact that one of the photographs in Henry M. Stanley's 1876 work, *Through the Dark Continent (Vol. 1),* (Harper Brothers) is of a Serombo King's palace lends credence to my assertion. The palace was thirty feet (about 9 meters) tall and stood on a base with a diameter of fifty-four feet (16.5 meters) (Njoh, 2007).

This begs an important question. Why has there always been a need to trivialize or disparage the accomplishments of Africans in urban and architectural development? Five plausible explanations come to mind. Firstly, devaluing the accomplishments of Africans in all domains was convenient and logical because it provided fodder for the myth of Africa as a "dark continent" that was later employed as a rationale for invading and colonizing the continent in the late 19th and 20th centuries. Secondly, the need to disparage indigenous African products, especially in the architectural and building industry was rooted in economics.

By discouraging indigenous African materials and correspondingly promoting the use of European varieties, colonial powers created markets for their products thereby stimulating their economies and increasing their profits from trade with colonies in Africa. Thirdly, disparaging African products while promoting European equivalents constitutes a form of cultural domination – a goal colonial authorities made no effort to even thinly veil. French colonial authorities, for instance, openly advertised their so-called civilizing mission *(mission civilisatrice)*, which was designed to "Frenchify" or "Europeanize" "cultural others." Articulating this philosophy in the human settlement space meant, for example, the imposition of European architectural styles, and norms on African societies, eroding indigenous cultural practices and identities. This cultural imposition has always served to strengthen Western or Eurocentric norms while suppressing African varieties in the built environment throughout the continent. Fourthly, disparaging indigenous African building and spatial organization concepts and practices in favor of Eurocentric equivalents facilitated political control of human settlements in the colonies. The imposition of Eurocentric architectural and spatial organization principles on Africans permitted European colonial powers to accomplish many colonial objectives. One of these was to shape the physical landscape of the colonies in line with their interests and priorities. Another was to consolidate their political control thereby furthering their colonial agendas. Furthermore, it allowed them to exert greater control over urban planning and infrastructure development. Finally, discouraging the use of indigenous building materials contributed to the dependency of African societies on European imports and technologies. This dependency reinforced the colonial economic system, making African economies reliant on European goods and services and perpetuating the unequal dynamics between colonizers and colonized.

At any rate, the myth of Africa as a continent without an urban history has no legs to stand on. Ancient history is richly laced with cities of great repute. Some of these already contained thousands, and in some cases, hundreds of thousands of inhabitants many years Before the Common Era (BCE). Noteworthy in this regard, are Zeila (also known as Seylac) in Somalia Thebes in Egypt, and Carthage in Tunisia. Zeila boasted 10,000 inhabitants by 1700 BCE. At its peak, the city-state of Carthage contained about half a million people (History, 2023, para. 3). Thebes (1500–1000 BCE), had a population of 75,000 and was Ancient Egypt's capital at some point. The influence of Thebes, as portrayed in George Modelski's meticulously compiled inventory of ancient cities, was not limited to Egypt and proximate regions. It was global, especially during the Amarna Period (1353–1336 BCE) when it was the world's most populous city (Modelski, 1997).

The city-state of Carthage came into existence in the 8th or 9th century BCE as a Phoenician settlement in what evolved to be contemporary Tunisia. It soon blossomed to reign as a major North African commercial hub for more than 500 years. During most of this time, it was known regionally and globally as a seafaring empire that played a dominant role in the copper, silver, gold, and textile market space. It was home to a protected harbor that included docking bays capable of handling hundreds of ships. As observed earlier, accounts of Africa's urban experience are flawed in many respects, particularly because they ignore, trivialize, or disparage the contribution of indigenous Africans to this inarguably rich history. Instead, the accounts tend to overstate the contribution of non-Africans, particularly Europeans and Arabs. Another shortcoming of the extant literature on African urban history is its inattentiveness to the interconnectedness among African cities and between them and their extra-continental peers. Furthermore, the accounts are oblivious to the importance of ethnicity, race, and class as analytical concepts in urban historical discourse. This Element in Global Urban History contributes to efforts to address these deficiencies. It does so at two levels; firstly, by proposing a periodization framework for analyzing African cities, and secondly, by employing the framework to analyze the cities from antiquity to the present.

1.2 A Periodized Compartmentalization of African Cities

Historiographers of cities in Africa have been relentless in their efforts to craft a typology for classifying African cities. Catherine Coquery-Vidrovitch (2009) expresses skepticism about initiatives that classify cities according to their origin or dominant features. She identifies the six-category typology of African cities proposed by some as an example of the wrong-headed nature of such initiatives. Criticizing such a typology as being reductionist, Coquery-Vidrovitch advances a case for frameworks that compartmentalize African cities chronologically or by major periods. Any attempt to discuss the urban experience in Africa according to specific periods can also prove challenging due to the varied timelines of urban development across the continent. The case for periodizing this history appears more persuasive. Hence, I propose a five-category periodization framework to analyze African cities.

The categories correspond with five main historical periods, namely Antiquity, including cities that emerged Before the Common Era to the 1st century in the Common Era (CE), Ancient Era, including cities created between the 2nd to 14th century CE, Era of Discovery, coinciding with Early African Civilization, including cities established between the 15th to late 19th century, Colonial Era, comprising cities created between the late 19th to early 20th centuries, and Postcolonial Era, including cities established between the early 20th century and the present.

Cities of Antiquity. Africa was already home to many cities of considerable size during the period Before the Common Era through the 1st century of the Common Era. Some of these cities, including, but not limited to, Faiyum, Alexandria, and Carthage, exist to date. Faiyum, reputed as the oldest continuously inhabited human settlement in Africa, was established in Egypt in 2181 BCE, while Alexandria, also in Egypt, was founded by Alexander the Great around 331 BCE, and Carthage was founded by Phoenicians in the 9th century BCE in present-day Tunisia.

Ancient Cities. Prominent among ancient African cities that were established during the Common Era are, Axum, Timbuktu, Great Zimbabwe, and Cairo. Major ancient cities in Ethiopia such as Gondar, home of the famous Ghebbi Castle (Figure 1), and Axum (or Aksum), which rose to become a major trading hub and a key player in the ancient trade among Africa, Arabia, and the Roman Empire, was established in Ethiopia in the 1st century CE. Timbuktu, which

Figure 1 The Fasil Ghebbi Castle, Gondar, Ethiopia.
Source: Wikimedia Commons (2023).

evolved to become a great center of Islamic learning, trade, and culture, was founded around the 5th century CE in present-day Mali. It was a key city in the Mali Empire and later, the Songhai Empire. Great Zimbabwe emerged around the 11th century CE in present-day Zimbabwe. Cairo, a megacity in present-day Egypt was established in 969 CE.

Africa's ancient cities, as discussed here, include those that emerged between the 1st century CE and 1300s. These can also be considered the continent's indigenous cities. As Satterthwaite (2021) noted, these were developed by indigenous Africans; some of them were still standing when European powers arrived to colonize the continent in the late 19th century. Satterthwaite lends credence to this assertion by contending as follows. "Most large African cities today were already well-established when colonial rule began to expand dramatically in the late 19th century" (para. 1). In sub-Saharan Africa, we find major historic cities such as the 700-year-old Malindi in Kenya (Figure 2), the 700-year-old Mbanza-Kongo in Angola, and the millennium-old Kano in Nigeria.

In North Africa, we find Fèz, which was founded in 786 CE in present-day Morocco, and Cairo, founded in 641 CE in present-day Egypt. As a testament to their global reach, some of these cities, such as Lagos and Porto Novo were major slave ports during the infamous Trans-Atlantic slave trade. Lagos, currently one of Africa's few megacities, evolved to become Nigeria's national capital during the first three decades of the country's postcolonial era (1961–1991). Porto Novo – locally known as Hogbonu or Ajashe – originated as

Figure 2 Malindi Town, Kenya today.
Source: Wikimedia Commons (2023).

a major tributary town of the Ancient Yoruba Kingdom of Oyo and evolved to become the national capital of the present-day Republic of Benin.

The Age of Discovery Cities or Early African Civilization. The early forays of Europeans into Africa date back to the mid 1300s, that is, about five centuries before the onset of the European colonial era in 1884/85. Branded as the Age of Discovery or Era of Exploration, the European incursions of this period had two main objectives: to set up trading posts and erect forts and castles in Africa. These evolved to constitute the nucleus around which vibrant human settlements developed, cities which were created during this era considered to be the continent's early civilization, grew, and proliferated. Some of them morphed into large human settlements that numbered among the most renowned cities in Africa before the Berlin Conference that officially launched the European colonial era in 1884/85.

Colonial Cities. These include the African cities that were created, or whose growth was influenced, by colonial powers in the late 19th to mid 20th century. European colonial powers established human settlements in selected areas of the continent to serve administrative, economic, and strategic purposes. As discussed later, these settlements were peculiar in many ways, but especially because of their colonial architectural styles and racially segregated physical structures. Colonial port cities such as Freetown, Sierra Leone; Dakar, Senegal; Johannesburg, South Africa; and Nairobi, Kenya are illustrative.

An important but seldom discussed form of human settlement that colonial powers introduced in Africa is the company town. Company towns remain part of the continent's landscape. European multinational corporations in the extractive industries such as mining and plantation agriculture were at the forefront of company town development projects. Often located near the mines or agricultural plantations, these towns served as centers for labor recruitment, accommodation, and services for workers in these industries. They outlived the colonial era, although many of them still retain features of their colonial past, including economic dependence on a single industry, limited infrastructure services, and unequal distribution. In the postcolonial period, many company towns continued to exist, with some transitioning to local or multinational ownership.

Thus, the towns, many of which have grown into large cosmopolitan towns, continue to grapple with the legacy of colonialism, economic dependency, and social inequality.

Postcolonial Cities. If nothing else, these cities are dynamic and evolving urban spaces that reflect the complexities of their checkered historical legacies, socio-economic transformations, and urbanization trends. These trends, because of their unprecedented rates, set African urban centers apart. Everywhere on the continent, rapid urbanization rates have outpaced the sluggish rate of public infrastructure development. This has led to critical deficiencies in different sectors, particularly health, education, and social welfare. At the same time, levels of unemployment continue to rapidly increase as more babies are added to the population every day. It is therefore no wonder that Africa ranks as the continent with the youngest population in the world. The continent's rapid population growth has placed immense pressure on urban infrastructure, housing, and related services, leading to problems such as urban sprawl, congestion, and severe quantitative deficiencies in the housing market. These have also led to the growth and proliferation of informal settlements throughout the continent.

1.3 Race, Ethnicity, and Class as Issues in Urban Africa

In ancient Egypt, the population included persons of Arabian, European, and Nubian extraction. Yet, race and ethnicity were nonissues in Ancient Egyptian society. On this subject, eminent historian of Ancient Africa, Frank Snowden (1991) stated that there was no color prejudice against Black Africans in antiquity. European colonialism ushered a new era marked by many changes in African built space; new building techniques and materials were introduced. So too were new laws governing spatial order. These changes were part of a meticulous plan on the part of European colonial authorities to dominate and control the built space. Racial spatial segregation was at the heart of this plan. Accordingly, colonial governments throughout the continent employed every pretext imaginable to enact policies that spatially segregated the races.

Class as a criterion for people's spatial location only became a feature of the built environment in Africa after the widespread demise of colonialism that occurred on the continent in the 1960s. Upon this demise, senior and mid-level members of the government bureaucracy moved speedily to take over the residential facilities vacated by colonial government officials. This effectively transformed what was racial spatial segregation during the colonial era into socio-economic spatial compartmentalization in the postcolonial-built space.

In addition to people of different socio-economic classes, the contemporary African city is home to many ethnic groups. Members of these groups are usually tied together by bonds that have been developed over many generations (Berman, 2010). The bonds are typically among persons with a common ancestry and/or geographic place of nativity such as a village or district. These tend to get stronger the further people are away from such a place. These bonds were reinforced during the colonial era. Colonial authorities used leaders of ethnic communities as extended arms of the municipal governance structure. In their bid to promote the economic interest of their home countries, colonial authorities created or actively encouraged many movements throughout the territories they controlled in Africa. In the southern African region, they recruited persons from distant locales to work in mines in South Africa. In the western and central African region, they recruited persons from hinterland areas to work in cash crop agricultural plantations on the coasts.

Once in the city, the newly arrived migrants typically seek out persons with whom they share either a common ancestry or hometown. During the colonial era, those who had arrived in the city earlier were expected to accommodate their newly arrived hometown compatriots. This often resulted in the formation of hometown associations (HTAs) and neighborhoods that contained persons from the same hometown (Njoh, 2006). A few examples of these include neighborhoods or whole urban districts such as the ethnic towns in Nigeria, including the Igbo Quarters (also known as Sabon Garri) in Jos, the Igbo Quarters in Bauchi, and the Hausa Quarters in Yoruba cities. In Nigeria's eastern neighbor, Cameroon, similar ethnic towns or districts also exist. Among these are, the famous Ibo Quarters, Hausa Quarters, Bamilike Street, and Meta Quarters in Kumba City, and the Hausa Quarters, also known as Abakwa or Stranger Quarters in Bamenda.

Stranger quarters and HTAs permit African urbanites to experience the sense of community that sociologists since the groundbreaking work of German sociologist, Ferdinand Tönnies 1887, had long associated with rural areas. This sense of community or Gemeinschaft – that is, what French sociologist, Emile Durkheim (1893/1933) called mechanical solidarity – is a feature of rural locales. In such places, in contrast to larger, urban, and industrial settings, family, kin and community ties are very strong, and people tend to not only look out but care, for each other. In a way, HTAs and stranger quarters constitute an African response to the problem of weakened and impersonalized ties, or what Tönnies called Gesellschaft, occasioned by urbanization. Thus, the typical African city knows two opposed types of ties, namely mechanical and organic. This latter is a product of the division of responsibilities and commensurate interdependence that occurs and creates a sense of solidarity among urbanites.

1.4 Element Outline

This Element contains seven sections. Section 2 follows this introduction and focuses on cities of the African Antiquity, including cities that emerged Before the Common Era through the 1st century CE. Section 3 focuses on the Urban Centers of Early African Civilization. These are cities that emerged between the 2nd and 14th centuries CE. Section 4 discusses African cities of the Era of Discovery or Age of Exploration. It concentrates on their origins and evolution as trading posts, their demographic composition, interconnectedness, and inter-action with other trading posts and indigenous towns. In Section 5, the focus is turned to cities that played important roles in the European colonial project (late 19th to early 20th centuries). Section 6 discusses an oft-ignored, but important variant of the colonial city – the company town – in Africa. Company towns were typically created by colonial corporations in the mining and plantation agricultural sectors to house their employees. Section 7, the final section, is dedicated to examining the postcolonial African city. This nomenclature not-withstanding, few of the cities were created during the postcolonial era. Many of them trace their origins to the colonial era or earlier. Thus, many of the cities classified as postcolonial here were around in some form during the widespread demise of colonialism in Africa in the 1960s.

2 Cities of African Antiquity

2.1 Introduction

Very little is known of cities of African antiquity, defined here as the period predating the Common Era. This is regrettable given that this period is replete with towns and cities of great repute. Although only the ruins of many of these cities remain as reminders of their once illustrious past, a few of them exist, if only significantly transformed, today. This section promotes an understanding of the best-known of these cities. Some of the cities owe their reputation to the critical roles they played as trading hubs and/or seats of governments for empires or kingdoms. Others owe theirs to their roles as centers of indigenous and received religions and spirituality. Therefore, to know these kingdoms is to understand the history of human settlement development and urbanization in general in Africa.

2.2 Major Antique African Cities

There is abundant evidence of Africa's rich urban history from Cape Town to Cairo, and from Dakar to Mogadishu. To understand Africa's main towns and cities is to appreciate the elements that kept the continent's antique kingdoms, empires, and cities alive, well, and strong. The continent has never known of a great kingdom without a town or city wherein lived its rulers, complete with well-structured governance systems, including the executive, judiciary, and policy-making bodies. Kingdoms and empires existed throughout the continent and can be categorized according to their geographic location, namely North, West, Center, and South. Figure 3 shows the major geographical locations of antique and ancient empires and kingdoms on the continent.

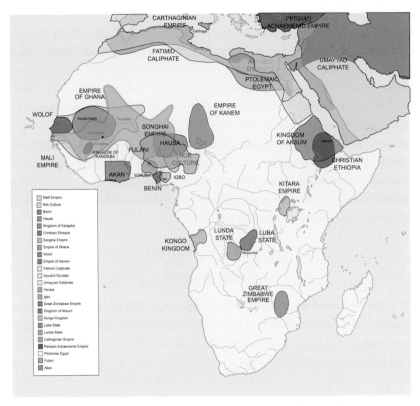

Figure 3 Major empires and kingdoms of ancient Africa.
Source: Wikimedia Commons.

North Africa of antiquity counted among its greatest kingdoms and empires, Egypt, Kush, and Carthage. Ancient Egypt, with Thebes as its capital for most of its existence, was home to some of the earliest, largest, and most meticulously structured kingdoms and human settlements. These developed and proliferated along the Valley of the Nile River around 3000 BCE. Within the cities that served multiple roles in each kingdom and beyond were well-organized governance systems, temples, sanitation infrastructure, communication systems, and residential facilities. Also worthy of note is the ancient city-state of Carthage whose ruins are in present-day Tunisia.

An entry in the *World Atlas* on the largest cities in ancient Egypt provides a succinct description of eight of Egypt's major ancient cities, including Memphis, Thebes, Amarna, Alexandria, Abydos, Elephantine, Nubt (Kom Ombo), and Hermopolis (World Atlas, 2023). These fell under two broad categories, the lower and upper regions, depending on their geographic location.

Accordingly, cities such as Memphis and Thebes that were in the north were classified as "upper" while cities like Alexandria located around the Mediterranean Sea were categorized as "lower." The cities were also classified according to their main roles in ancient Egyptian societies. Thus, while many played mainly politico-administrative roles, some were primarily religious centers, while others played both roles. There is a tendency among historiographers of cities in Africa, to acknowledge the influence of Islam while ignoring that of indigenous African religions on the emergence and growth of ancient African cities. This is true even for some of the most seasoned of these historiographers such as Coquery-Vitdrovitch (2009). Her otherwise meticulously researched and well-written book, *The History of African Cities South of the Sahara,* contains a whole section on the influence of Islam on African Cities but none on the impact of indigenous African religions or spirituality. Yet, both religions significantly contributed to the emergence and growth of ancient African cities. While great ancient human settlements such as the city-state of Kano in Nigeria, and Great Zimbabwe in present-day Zimbabwe originated as indigenous African spiritual centers, others such as Fez in contemporary Morocco emerged as Islamic centers. My focus in this section is exclusively on the African cities that emerged Before the Common Era. These can be grouped by geo-political regions, namely North Africa and Sub-Saharan Africa.

2.2.1 North Africa

Evidence of many cities that emerged Before the Common Era in Africa has been found mainly, but not exclusively in the northern part of the continent. Five of these, Memphis, Faiyum, Thebes, Amarna, and Carthage are illustrative. These cities significantly impacted not only their geographically proximate neighbors but also human settlements elsewhere. As shown in the following passage, the cities attained fame as international religious, political, and cultural centers.

The Antique City of Memphis. Founded by King Menes in 3150 BCE, Memphis exemplified cities that were influential as major centers of politico-administration and religion. Figure 4 shows some of the Ruins of this antique city. They are the ruins of Hypostyle Hall and Pylon of Ramses II in Mit-Rahineh, Memphis. Located at the entrance to the Nile River Valley around the Giza plateau, this city served as Egypt's pioneer capital from 2950 BCE to 2180 BCE. As a religious center, Memphis was home to the Temple of Ptah, one of the most renowned temples in ancient Egypt. The temple was created in honor of the ancient god of Ptah believed to be a creator god and a patron of artisans. Thanks to its location along the River Nile, communication between Memphis

Figure 4 Ruins of the Hypostyle Hall and Pylon of Ramses II
in Mit-Rahineh, Memphis.

Source: Wikimedia Commons.

and other places were easy, which is one reason why traffic in and out of the city was commonplace. Also commonplace, were traces of foreign influence, the most conspicuous of which is the city's name. Memphis, noted the *World History Encyclopedia,* is a Greek translation of the city's indigenous name, *Mennefer,* which means, "the enduring and beautiful" (WHE, 2023). Memphis was also known for its teeming population; it boasted a population of at least 30,000 during its infancy between 3150 BCE and 1400 BCE.

The Antique City of Faiyum. Founded in about 2181 BCE, this city holds the prize of first place as the oldest continuously inhabited human settlement in all of Africa. It is located about 100 kilometers southwest of Egypt's capital, Cairo. In its heydays in ancient times, the city was an important center of religion, politics, trade, and agriculture. Prominent among the many temples attesting to its history as a religious center are the Temple of Sobek and the Temple of Hathor. Its fertile soil permitted it to produce enough food to supply its growing population and export some to neighboring places. Today, Faiyum is known globally for its touristic value; it is a favorite destination for researchers interested in Africa's rich urban history, culture, and aesthetic beauty.

The Antique City of Thebes. This is another ancient Egyptian city of high acclaim. It stood tall among cities of the Amarna Period in Egypt (1353–1336 BCE) as a bustling hub and locale of religious and politico-administrative affairs. In his illuminating entry on Thebes in *World History Encyclopedia,* Joshua

Mark characterized the city in its heydays as covering an area of 93 square kilometers or 36 square miles (Mark, 2016). Like Memphis, Thebes was also located along the River Nile, approximately 800 kilometers or 500 miles from the Mediterranean Sea, and some 675 kilometers or 419 miles south of Cairo. The ruins sitting as a glaring reminder of this great ancient city's irrefutable existence can be found in the cities of Luxor and Karnak in contemporary Egypt (Figure 5). Known as Waset to ancient Egyptians, Thebes derived its fame from many of its attributes, including the fact that it was the main city of the fourth Upper Egyptian *Nome (Sceptre nome)*; at the same time, it served as the capital of Egypt for extended periods during the Middle Kingdom and New Kingdom eras (about 1570–1069 BCE).

The Antique City of Amarna. This city was originally named Akhenaten when it was established in 1346 BCE; Amarna is its modern Arabic name. Located between the ancient Egyptian capitals of Memphis and Thebes, Amarna was one of the cities that served as the seat of the Egyptian government in ancient times. It was the capital under Pharoah Akhenaten (1353–1336 BCE), a powerful Egyptian king with an unbridled propensity for self-absorbance. This propensity was evident in the fact that he ordered the creation of a new capital city, Akhenaten, which he named after himself and in honor of the sun god, Aten.

Figure 5 Thebes Necropolis.
Source: SFEC_AEH_-ThebesNecropolis-2010-RamsesIII045.jpg: Steve F-E-Cameron.

Thus, he was responsible for the controversial decision that relocated ancient Egypt's capital from Memphis to Amarna. It is therefore no wonder that upon his demise in 1332 BCE, the seat of the Egyptian government was relocated back to Memphis. This resulted in, among other things, the abandonment and subsequent demise of Amarna.

The Antique City of Carthage. This city originated as a Canaanite Phoenician colony on the east of Lake Tunis in present-day Tunisia. It is said to have been founded by the Phoenicians of Tyre in 814 BCE and was named Carthage, which simply means "new town" in Phoenician. From its seemingly routine beginning, the city evolved to become one of the largest, most famous, and wealthiest cities of the classical world (see Figure 6). It derived this reputation and fame from its role mainly as a thriving port city and trading hub of the Ancient Mediterranean region. That Carthage rose to play an important role as a hub of international trade did not happen by chance. Rather, as Patrick Hunt (2017) noted, the Phoenicians exercised much care in selecting sites, especially for their maritime colonies. They prioritized the quality of harbors and their proximity to trade routes. The decision to locate Carthage on a promontory on the coast was intended to afford it influence and control over ships passing between Sicily and the North African coast as they traversed the Mediterranean Sea.

Figure 6 Bird's eye view of ancient Carthage.

Source: Wikimedia Commons: https://commons.wikimedia.org/wiki/File:Carthage, _Missouri_1891_LOC_gm71005353.jpg.

2.2.2 Sub-Saharan Africa

Going by the contemporary literature on the historiography of African cities one would be forgiven for thinking that the sub-Saharan African region had no large human settlements predating the Common Era. According to this literature, cities that emerged Before the Common Era were restricted to the Northern part of the continent. A few exceptions are, however, noteworthy. Richard Hull's brief text on African Cities and Towns before the European Conquest includes a map that lists "major cities of Eastern and Southern Africa from 591 BCE to the 19th century" (Hull, 1976, p. 30). On her part, Catherine Coquery-Vidrovitch's copious work on The History of African Cities South of the Sahara includes narratives on cities of the Great African Antiquity such as Meroe and Axum that were based in the sub-Saharan region (Coquery-Vidrovitch, 2009). Meroe was already involved in iron metallurgy by the 4th century BCE. Despite this, the only cities of the Great African Antiquity that are often discussed in the relevant literature are those of North Africa.

One possible reason for this is North Africa's proximity to Europe and the Middle East. Thus, North Africa's antique cities were likely to be more exposed to foreign travelers from Europe and Arabia than their sub-Saharan counterparts. Yet, there is unimpeachable evidence pointing to the presence of many important human settlements in the sub-Saharan Africa region, far removed from both the Mediterranean and Egypt. Examples of these settlements include Adulis, Axum, Karmah, Kumbi Saleh, Djenné-Djenno, Meroe, and Napata.

The Antique City-State of Adulis. Located on the coast of the Red Sea, this city-state of African antiquity existed between the period of late antiquity and early medieval times. It enjoyed its peak period of influence from around the 1st to the 7th century CE. During this period, it flourished as a prominent trading center and port city on the Red Sea, serving as a crucial link between various civilizations of the Mediterranean, Arabia, the Indian Ocean, and the African hinterland. It took advantage of its location to facilitate the exchange of ideas, cultures, and goods such as ivory, gold, spices, incense, and exotic animals. Recent archaeological evidence suggests that the city contained people who were highly skilled in pottery, arts, and architecture. By the official onset of the European colonial era in Africa, Adulis had lost some of its fame and allure. Several factors accounted for this, prominent among which were changes in trade routes, the emergence of competing trading centers such as Axum in the proximate region, political instability, and adverse environmental conditions.

The Antique City of Axum. Also known as Aksum, this city served as the capital of the Aksumite Kingdom in what is present-day Ethiopia. Although it became famous from the 1st century CE to the 7th century CE, it likely emerged

Before the Common Era. It became famous by taking advantage of its strategic geographic location on the highlands of northern Ethiopia, near the Red Sea coast. This location permitted it to serve as a vital hub for trade routes connecting Africa, the Mediterranean world, and the Indian Ocean. In its heydays, Axum thrived as a trading center, benefiting from its access to trade routes linking it with regions such as Arabia, India, Egypt, and the Roman Empire. It traded goods such as ivory, gold, spices, and exotic animals. It derived some of its fame from its architectural ingenuity. In this regard, it boasted some of the most iconic structures of its day. Foremost among these were its massive stone obelisks, some of which stood over 24-meters tall. These were designed to mark graves, symbolize royal power, and articulate religious authority. Unlike many African cities of that era, Axum played a significant role in the early spread of Christianity in the region. It was one of the earliest Christian kingdoms, with the religion gaining prominence as early as the 4th century CE. The city contributed enormously to making Ethiopian Christianity one of the oldest in the world. Contemporary Axum, a shadow of its historic self, remains a vibrant touristic destination where people go to view the ruins, remnants, or replicas of ancient royal palaces and tombs of Aksumite kings, queens, and nobles. It is a UNESCO World Heritage Site.

The Antique City of Djenné-Djenno. One of the oldest known cities in sub-Saharan Africa, this city which dates to the days of the Mali and Songhai empires, is, as noted in the *Encyclopedia Britannica* (2023), located near the locale of the ruins of a town, Djenné-Djenno (or Jenne-Jeno) whose origins have been traced to antiquity (about 250 BCE). It was situated on the floodplains of the area between the Bani River and River Niger, about 354 kilometers (220 miles) southwest of Timbuktu. It served as a major trade center, particularly for the trans-Saharan trading system. Djenné-Djenno was characterized by its mud-brick architecture and is considered one of the earliest urban centers in the region. It was established between the 8th and 13th centuries and evolved to become a leading center of Islamic learning and culture from the 13th to the 17th centuries. In its heydays, Djenné had grown to become an entrepôt between the traders of the central and western Sudan and their counterparts in Guinea's tropical forest region. Its fame was due to two main factors; the first was its direct connection by river with Timbuktu and from its location at the head of the trade routes to the gold mines of Bitou (in present-day Côte d'Ivoire), to Lobé, and to Bouré. The second is the fact that it was an important entrepôt for salt. With the defeat of the Songhai Empire by Moroccan forces in the 16th century, the town fell under Moroccan rule.

The Antique City of Karmah (or Kerma). The Encyclopedia Britannica (2024) contains a succinct entry on Karmah. This city of African antiquity was located along the River Nile, about 300 kilometers north of present-day Khartoum, the capital of contemporary Sudan. It was the capital of the Kingdom of Kush during the New Kingdoms of ancient Egypt (around 2500–1500 BCE). At the same time, it was an important center for trade, agriculture, and religion, controlling lucrative trade routes along the Nile. It was one of the earliest and most powerful civilizations in northeastern Africa. Archaeological evidence reveals that the city did not develop spontaneously. Rather, its development was based on a meticulous preconceived urban design. This included a central administrative and, religious complex, surrounded by residential areas and agricultural lands. The evidence also revealed a sophisticated urban center, including monumental architecture and defensive walls. The central complex included a royal palace and an administrative center, temples, and other structures associated with the ruling elite.

Karmah wielded influence not only over its proximate neighbors but also over distant cities and regions. This is because it was a center of religious and cultural activity, with temples dedicated to the worship of local and regional deities. Its rulers were viewed as divine kings or priest-kings, and religion played a central role in the organization of the society writ large. In addition, because of its strategic location, the city served as a trading hub for goods such as gold, ivory, ebony, and other luxury items between the African hinterland and Northern Africa, and Arabia.

The Antique City of Koumbi Saleh. Consensus is lacking concerning when Koumbi (or Kumbi) Saleh emerged as a human settlement. However, most accounts state that it commanded fame from the 9th to the 11th century CE (Hatshetpsut, 2024). Other sources have recorded the 1st century CE as the period when the city rose to fame (Wikipedia, 2024). It was part of the Ghana Kingdom, which is also believed to have come into existence at about that same time. Therefore, it is conceivable that the city's emergence predated the Common Era. For this reason, I treat it here as one of Africa's human settlements of Antiquity.

This city was located some 322 kilometers (200 miles) north of modern Bamako in Mali. In addition to being the Ghana Kingdom's capital, Koumbi Saleh served as its commercial and industrial hub. Hence, it is there that the indigenous techniques for gold mining and iron works for which the kingdom was well-known were developed and refined. Concerning international commerce, the city played a crucial role in the trans-Sahara gold trade. It also served as a market for trading products from the kingdom and other areas. Koumbi Saleh was the locale for developing and refining the industrial techniques and tools that made the Ghana Kingdom famous; it was also the venue for trading locally produced gold for salt from the Sahara Desert.

Back in the eleventh century, a Spanish Muslim named, Al-Bakri, had written about Koumbi Saleh. He described the city as comprised of two towns 10 kilometers (6 miles) apart; one of these was inhabited by Muslim merchants while the other was home to the kingdom's monarch. This latter town, named El-Ghaba, was enclosed within a stone wall that mainly reinforced security around the king. The two towns were connected by a stretch of land occupied by sparsely distributed residential buildings. Over time some in-filling took place and resulted in a merger of the two towns. Thus, the fact that the two have always been viewed as one.

Koumbi Saleh played multifaceted roles; it was the spiritual, economic, and administrative or royal capital of the kingdom. As the religious capital, it contained a sacred grove of trees that served Soninke's religious purposes. The trees also enclosed the king's palace, which was the most magnanimous structure in the city. This suggests that the strategy of using size as an expression of power in built space that was widely employed during the European colonial era in Africa predated the era by several centuries. Another testament to the city's religious role is the fact that it contained a mosque reserved for visiting Muslims. The mosque was located in El-Ghaba, the main part of the city. The other part was equipped with freshwater wells that encircled the town. It was also richly punctuated with vegetable gardens. In addition, and as a further testament to its religious role, it contained a dozen mosques. One of these was used for Friday prayers and hosted scholars, scribes, and Islamic jurists. The mosques were in areas that doubled as business districts. This was mainly because the town's Muslim residents were mostly merchants.

As a commercial town, Koumbi Saleh positioned itself to extract economic benefits from the trans-Sahara trade in gold, copper, salt, textiles, and leather. In addition, the kingdom instituted a meticulous taxation system that charged merchants one gold dinar on imports of salt and two on exports of the same. Concerning its governance structure, the kingdom was highly centralized. It had a core region that was surrounded by vassal states. Several minor kings functioned under the authority of the supreme monarch. The minor kings were known as *kofu* – a Mandinka word for junior king. They oversaw territorial units. With time, most of the administrative positions in the kingdom were occupied by Muslims.

The Antique City of Meroë. This city was located about 200 kilometers northeast of contemporary Khartoum in present-day Sudan. At the time, the general region was known as Nubia and constituted part of the Great Kingdom of Kush. Meroe was the capital of this Kingdom and part of a powerful civilization that flourished between the 8th century BCE and the 4th century CE. It was a vibrant trade hub that took advantage of its strategic location, connecting sub-Saharan Africa with Egypt, the wider Mediterranean world, and the Red Sea region. It profited from trade routes that crossed the Nile and stretched into the heart of Africa. It derived most of its fame from its advanced ironworking industry. The region was rich in iron ore, and the Kushites had mastered iron smelting techniques, producing high-quality iron goods, including weapons, tools, and jewelry. Also, it was famous for its pyramids, which served as royal burial sites for Kushite kings and queens. The pyramids are distinguishable from their Egyptian counterparts because they are smaller and steeper.

Culturally, Meroë served as an important religious center, indulging in both indigenous African religion and the religious practices of ancient Egypt. The Kushite kings adopted many Egyptian customs and deities, although they also worshipped local gods. Some of the cultural artifacts of the Kushites, such as the writing system known as the Meroitic script exist to date. The Kingdom of Kush began experiencing a decline around the 4th century CE due to various factors not least of which were governmental changes, economic shifts, and invasions by neighboring powers.

The Antique City of Napata. This is an important city of the African antiquity. Located along the Nile River in what is today Sudan, the city's period of prominence as the capital of Kush dates to around the 8th century BCE and continued until about the 4th century CE. It served as a significant political and religious center, particularly during the period of the Kingdom of Kush of African antiquity. Like many cities that rose to fame at the time, Napata was located on the bank of the Nile River; it was some 400 kilometers north of present-day Khartoum in Sudan. Thanks to its strategic location along a major navigable river, it became a vital hub for trade and commerce. It also played a crucial politico-administrative role as the capital of the Kingdom of Kush at various periods in its history. The kingdom was ruled by a succession of Kushite kings and queens, often referred to as Pharaohs. These rulers propelled Napata to great heights as the political and administrative center of their realm. The city was home to royal palaces, administrative buildings, and temples dedicated to the kingdom's gods and goddesses. Napata was not only a politico-administrative center; it doubled as a major cultural and religious center as it was home to temples dedicated to various deities, with the cult of Amun being foremost.

2.3 Conclusion

The history of Africa is replete with accounts of towns and cities of great repute. These were typically capitals of influential kingdoms, empires, and caliphates dating to antiquity. The cities were not only of national, but also of regional and international importance as religious and/or trade centers. Paradoxically, these cities were not as unique as conventional narratives may suggest. Rather, they bore a striking resemblance to their counterparts in Europe at the time. Like cities in Europe and other parts of the world, those in Africa experienced ebbs and flows with the kingdoms or empires of which they were a part. They derived their fame from the same sources as these kingdoms or empires. Among these sources were trade, agriculture, government administration, and scholarship. Evidence of the role of these towns and cities abounds. However, what is rare is concrete evidence of their spatial structure. This is because the sites of many of them have survived only in fragments. For a few, particularly those that exist to date, they have been continuously inhabited, and have evolved to assume different forms, and sometimes, functions.

3 Urban Centers of Early African Civilization

3.1 Introduction

Africa boasts a rich urban history dating to antiquity as discussed in the previous section. This section focuses on the continent's ancient cities, including human settlements established between the 2nd and 14th centuries CE. This discussion renders disingenuous, at best, claims that Africa had no history of urbanization predating the arrival of the European conquest. Such all-too-familiar claims were often made to buttress the myth of Africa as a "dark continent." This was employed by Europeans as a rationale to invade and colonize the continent in the late 19th century. This myth also characterizes Africa as a continent without a history of architecture and human settlement development.

However, the myth runs counter to ancient architectural monuments that exist to date; one example is the monarch's Obelisks at Aksum, Ethiopia, which is about 24 meters (or 79 feet) tall. There is also no shortage of analysts and observers who have been mesmerized by the sophistication of indigenous African spatial design. The following entry in a Dutch explorer's diary in 1602 in which he compared Benin City in present-day Nigeria to Amsterdam, Holland, is illustrative.

> The town seemeth to be great; when you enter into it, you go into a great broad street, not paved, which seems to be seven or eight times broader than Warmoes Street in Amsterdam; which goeth right out and never crooks . . . ; it is thought that that street is a mile long. When you are on the great street aforesaid, you see many great streets on the sides thereof, which go right forth . . . . The houses in this town stand in good order, one close and even with the other, as the houses in Holland stand . . . . The King's Court is very great, within it having many great four-square plains, which round about them have galleries, "wherein there is always watch kept" (Tordoff, 1984: 29–30).

This, and the material presented in the previous section constitute unimpeachable evidence that large human settlements – particularly towns and cities – were already well-established in Africa before the formal onset of the European colonial era in 1884/85. These towns came mainly in two varieties.

The first was created by Africans themselves (the indigenous towns), and the second included towns that were created by Europeans to serve as trading posts. This section identifies and discusses the most prominent of these towns.

3.2 Early African Urban Centers

Africa boasts many ancient cities that exist to date. Many of these cities are in the Maghrib or North Africa region and were discussed in Section 1. Hence, apart from passing mention of the ancient North African cities, this section focuses mainly on ancient sub-Saharan African cities. Prominent among the continent's ancient cities are Alexandria, Cairo, and Faiyum (in Egypt); Tunis in Tunisia; and Fes and Marrakech in Morocco. Similar ancient cities exist in sub-Saharan Africa, and include, Axum, Lalibela, and Gondar in Ethiopia; Djenné in Mali; Benin and Kano in Nigeria, Mbanza-Kongo in Angola, and Mombasa in Kenya.

Alexandria, Egypt. In their encyclopedic entry on this city, Michael Reimer and colleagues (2023) drew attention to its Arabic appellation, namely Al-Iskandariyyah – perhaps as a stark reminder of its conquest by Arabs in 642 CE. Alexandria (Figure 7) is believed to have been founded by Alexander the Great in 332 BCE. It is located on the Mediterranean coast at the western edge of the Nile River delta some 183 kilometers (about 114 miles) northwest of Cairo

Figure 7 Contemporary Alexandria.
Source: https://commons.wikimedia.org/wiki/File:Alexandria2.jpg.

in Lower Egypt. It has always maintained a high profile nationally, regionally, and internationally. Like Memphis, it served as the seat of the Egyptian government at some point – the Greco-Roman period, to be precise. It was the national capital of Egypt from its founding in 332 BCE until the 7th century when it was defeated by the Arabs. This is also when Alexandria lost its politico-administrative dominance to Cairo, which became the new seat of the Egyptian national government. Despite this, the city maintained its dominance in other areas until the late-15th century.

Throughout its ancient history, Alexandria was reputed as a commercial hub and cultural trendsetter in the general region of Egypt. By some accounts, the city was once the cultural headquarters of the ancient world, surpassing Athens, Greece which was a well-known European cultural icon of the time. Alexandria was also known for its crucial role in preserving and transmitting Hellenic culture not only to the Mediterranean region but also to other parts of the world. It was, in the immutable words of one analyst, a crucible of scholarship, piety, and ecclesiastical politics in early Christian history (Reimer et al., 2023, para. 2). Right into the twilight of the 15th century, Alexandria remained an important hub of maritime commerce, a regional and international center of naval operations, a reputable center of exotic craft production, and an important transit point in trade between the Mediterranean Basin and the Red Sea.

However, by the 16th century, Alexandria began witnessing some decline particularly because it was hit by several unforeseen negative eventualities, not least of which were an epidemic disease breakout, administrative ineptitude, and sheer neglect. By the end of the 18th century, most of the city's dazzling splendor was gone and it had become a mere shadow of its once illustrious self. Thus, what French troops found when they invaded Egypt in 1798 was the inglorious, as opposed to the celebrated, Alexandria of the pre-18th century. What they found was a tiny decrepit town of some 10,000 inhabitants.

3.3 West Africa

This is home to many of the most famous kingdoms and empires in ancient Africa. Most of these were in the Sahel region, bounded on the north by the Sahara Desert and on the south by the rain forests. Prominent among these empires was the Ghana Kingdom – not to be confused with the present-day Republic of Ghana. This kingdom thrived between the 9th and 13th century CE; it was built by the Soninke people and was in the area currently occupied by Mauritania and Mali. The emergence of the kingdom in the 9th century marked the beginning of a series of vibrant West Africa-based empires and kingdoms, foremost among which were Mali and Songhay.

Figure 8 Drawing of Benin City prior to its destruction by the British in 1897. **Source:** Wikimedia Commons.

The Ancient Kingdom of Benin, Nigeria. A major gap in the history of urbanization in Africa is the scant attention that it has afforded Benin City. Yet, as shown in Figure 8, the history of this city is as rich as that of any other ancient human settlement in Africa. Like most ancient cities on the continent, Benin served as the seat of government for a great kingdom, the Kingdom of Benin. This was established in the 11th century and flourished as a well-organized, sophisticated, and powerful kingdom whose dominion extended to many parts of present-day southern Nigeria. Also, like many ancient cities, Benin City actively participated in trade, commerce, and societal governance. Concerning trade, it was reputed as a center of trade for brass and ivory products, all products that were considered hot commodities, especially by European traders. The kingdom attained its pinnacle during the reign of King (or Oba) Ewuare the Great (1440–1473); he significantly extended the kingdom's dominion to cover many parts of contemporary south and southeastern Nigeria.

Despite its level of development, Benin remained relatively unknown to the rest of the world for a long time. The first Europeans did not contact Benin until the 15th century. This is when the Portuguese established trade relations with the Benin Kingdom and set in motion a mutually beneficial exchange of goods and cultural influences. Observers of the time were unified in characterizing the city as wealthy, peaceful, secure, and safe; some compared it to London, which, at the time suffered from serious problems such as thievery, prostitution, filth, and inadequate housing. In contrast, ancient Benin City was so safe that there was never any need for inhabitants to bother locking their doors at any time.

Ancient Benin City was sophisticated not only in terms of its institutional framework but also concerning its architecture and spatial structure. Writing in the online edition of the Guardian, Mawuna Koutini characterized the city during ancient times as well-planned, by rules of symmetry. It counted among the earliest human settlements to have something that resembled streetlights. Lourenço Pinto a Portuguese explorer who visited the city in 1485 is said to have remarked in his diary that Benin City was larger than major European cities of the time (Koutini, 2016). It was, the explorer went on, larger than Lisbon, which was Europe's most prominent city then. Movement within the city was facilitated by a system of streets that intersected at right angles; some of the streets went as far as the naked eye could see.

In the 13th century, the city was fitted with massive enclosure walls to protect it against external threats. The walls were nothing short of an engineering marvel at the time! They were, as Koutini (2016) described them, four times longer than the Great Wall of China, and consumed a hundred times more material than the Great Pyramid of Cheops. In his very illuminating piece in the New Scientist, Fred Pearce described the layout of ancient Benin City as containing many smaller walls that separated the city into some 500 distinct villages (Pearce, 1992). The walls extended for more than 16,000 kilometers (about 9,942 miles) and circumscribed more than 500 interconnected settlement boundaries.

Ghana Kingdom. The Ghana Kingdom was richly endowed with gold and well-known for its ingenuity in gold mining, iron crafts, and weapon production. Its abundant reserves of gold earned it the nickname, "land-of-gold." According to one analyst, "it was a powerful trading empire," which experienced its heydays between 600 CE and 1200 CE. Rather early in the kingdom's evolution, its kings had developed and institutionalized an effective system of taxation, which ensured the collection of taxes on all goods and services passing through the territory under the kingdom's auspices. As a highly centralized kingdom, all politico-administrative decisions regarding the kingdom's welfare were taken in its capital city, Koumbi Saleh.

Niani, Timbuktu, Gao, Djenné, and Walata in the Mali Kingdom. Like many of the empires in ancient West Africa, the Mali Kingdom – not to be confused with the contemporary Republic of Mali – thrived on commerce. Established by the powerful Malinke king, King Sundiata Keita, the Mali Kingdom, which was located near the Upper Niger River, existed between the 13th and 16th centuries. In its characterization of this extremely wealthy kingdom and its equally rich king, a succinct article in *National Geographic* (2023) underscored the following. The kingdom was considerably vast in terms of its geographic expanse; it covered territories fully or partially occupied today by as many as nine African countries, including Mali, Senegal, the Gambia, Guinea, Niger, Nigeria, Chad, Mauritania, and Burkina Faso. The kingdom flourished from the 13th to the 16th century and witnessed its heydays during the reign of King Mansa Musa I (1312 CE to 1337 CE). King Musa was a very wealthy monarch who invested significantly in the kingdom's main cities, including Niani, Timbuktu, Gao, Djenné, and Walata.

The king was known to invite architects and urban designers from different parts of the world to contribute to the design of new spatial and physical structures. Upon returning from Mecca, Mansa Musa embarked on a project to revitalize human settlements throughout his kingdom. As part of this, he built mosques, and large public buildings in the legendary cities of Niani, Gao, Timbuktu, and Djenné.

The Ancient City of Niani. This once thriving capital of the wealthy Kingdom of Mali is today a small village. It is located on the left bank of River Sankarani, a tributary of River Niger in the northeastern part of the contemporary Republic of Guinea. In ancient times, it was designated the capital of the Mali Kingdom by its Mandingo (Malinke) founder, King Sundiata Keita (also known as Mari Djata). He led the kingdom from about 1250 CE to 1255 CE. Niani remained the capital, flourished, and became the kingdom's commercial, and industrial center. This was especially due to its coastal location on the Atlantic coast. This afforded the kingdom access to the Atlantic Ocean. It is thanks to Niani that the Mali Kingdom is on record as an active participant in the infamous trans-Atlantic slave trade. Its strategic location also made it a vibrant market for hot commodities of the time, including gold, salt, and kola nuts.

The Ancient City of Gao. Founded by fishermen in the 7th century (CE), Gao is located along River Niger at the southern edge of the Sahara Desert approximately 300 kilometers (200 miles) southeast of Timbuktu. In ancient times, it comprised mainly Songhai people and took advantage of its location on a river highway, the Niger River, to play a dominant role as a trading center. It was one of the best-known trading centers for gold, copper, and salt as well as slaves in western Africa at that time. It evolved to become the capital of the Songhai Empire in the early 11th century and was later annexed by the Mali Kingdom in 1325 CE. In about 1365 CE, Songhai regained control over Gao. The city experienced a sharp decline in its stature after 1591 when Morocco ended Songhai's rule in the region.

The Ancient Kingdom of Songhay. Chronologically, the Kingdom of Songhay and that of Mali overlapped. Both existed between 1350 CE and 1600 CE although at some point, the Songhay Kingdom overpowered and annexed parts of the Mali Kingdom. Two of the rulers of Songhay, Sonni Ali, and Mohammed Askia stand out as the most influential throughout the kingdom's history. Sonni Ali ascended to the throne of the kingdom in 1464 CE. Among his foremost accomplishments with implications for urbanization are the following three. Firstly, he transformed the kingdom's capital, Gao, into an important regional and international center of commerce as well as Islamic culture and learning. Secondly, he seized and incorporated into the Songhay Kingdom, cities such as Timbuktu and Djenné, which were previously controlled by the Kingdom of Mali. Finally, he was avowedly dedicated to making Songhay a great empire. Sonni's successor, Mohammed Askia, who unlike him was a devout Muslim, continued in his footsteps but proceeded to ensure the integration of religion and commerce in the kingdom. Sonni is most notable because once he ascended to the throne in 1493 CE, he invested significantly in urban development, expanded the kingdom, and set up a more meticulous and highly centralized governance structure. In addition, he brought peace and stability to the kingdom, developed a new system of laws, and invested considerably in the military and education.

The Ancient Kanem-Bornu Empire. This empire existed from the 9th to the 19th century. It was ruled by the Sef (also known as Sayf, and Sefawa) Dynasty, and like most of the empires and kingdoms in Africa at that time, was linked to the rest of the world through trade. At the peak of its reign, the empire encompassed territories constituting parts of contemporary countries such as southern Chad, northern Cameroon, northeastern Nigeria, eastern Niger, and southern Libya. The empire's contribution to Africa's urban history was through human settlements especially the capital city that their kings established and maintained over time. The capital city of the Kanem-Bornu Empire was Njimi; this was established in the 11th century in the northeast of Lake Chad. This location was quite strategic especially because of its proximity to a massive body of freshwater, Lake Chad. The location was also strategic from a geographic perspective as it permitted the city to play a dominant role in the trans-Saharan trade in ivory, salt, and slaves.

The Ancient City of Timbuktu, Mali. Although Niani was the capital of the Mali Kingdom, Timbuktu was its most important city. While the city exists to date, it has long lost its ancient allure and stature. Located on the southern edge of the Sahara Desert, some 13 kilometers (about 8 miles) north of the Niger River in the contemporary Republic of Mali, Timbuktu evolved to become an important center of Islamic learning and culture from the 1400s to the 1600s. It is home to three of the oldest mosques in West Africa. Built between the 14th and 15th centuries, at least three hundred years before the European colonial era, these mosques include Djinguereber, Sankore, and Sidi Yahia. Also, the city commanded much importance in the kingdom and broader Sahelian region for two main reasons. The first was its proximity to a great water highway, the Niger River, and the second is the fact that it was the starting point of the trans-Saharan camel caravans that transported products from the region northwards.

3.4 Central Africa

Kongo was one of the largest and most organized constituted states in the central and southern Africa region from the 14th to the 19th centuries. Located south of the River Congo, this kingdom was founded in the 1500s and remained active through the 19th century. Thus, its founding was of more recent vintage in comparison to the known ancient empires of West and North Africa. The kingdom's dominion extended to encompass parts of contemporary Angola, Congo (DRC), and Congo (PRC).

The Ancient City of Mbanza Kongo. The urban experience of the Central Africa region revolved around its largest town and capital city, Mbanza Kongo, and its five powerful provinces, including Soyo, Mbata, Nsundi, Mpangu, and Mpemba. The strategic location of the capital city on a 570-meter-high plateau along a river highway, the Congo River, facilitated its role as the dominant administrative and commercial town in the kingdom. Thus, Mbanza Kongo was not only the political capital, it was also the commercial and spiritual hub of the kingdom. Like the other coastal African empires and kingdoms of the time, Kongo played an active role in the infamous trans-Atlantic trade of enslaved Africans.

Its spatial structure was thought-provoking; the king's palace, the royal funeral places, the customary court, and the holy tree constituted the nucleus around which the town's historical area grew. As an ancient spiritual town in sub-Saharan Africa, Mbanza Kongo stands out for one paradoxical reason. It contained Christian artifacts, including churches constructed according to European standards. This paradox is due especially to the fact that the head of this kingdom at the heart of Africa had converted to Roman Catholicism as far back as 1491. Thanks to this, Mbanza Kongo was renamed Sao Salvador, and a cathedral, the Cathedral of Sao Salvador (after the town's new name) was erected there in 1549. Through the king's conversion to Christianity, the construction of the cathedral, and ancillary monumental Christian structures, Mbanza Kongo was inserted into the heart of European power. Thenceforth, and operating out of the city under its Catholic Christian name, Sao Salvador, the king was able to send his own ambassadors to the Vatican and the King's Court in Portugal.

Over time, Sao Salvador increasingly evolved to bear if only a passing resemblance to vintage European cities. This, as noted in the UNESCO Heritage Convention report (UNESCO, 2023), is due to the early involvement of the Portuguese in the town's urban development initiatives. Here, the Portuguese had moved speedily to add European-style stone buildings including many churches to the existing urban conurbation built of local materials by indigenous technicians. By the onset of the European colonial era in the 19th century, Mbanza Kongo had experienced physical and demographic growth.

The population at the time had become unmistakably cosmopolitan with many Christians and local elites, who never renounced their traditional religious practices. Archaeological evidence revealed that despite foreign cultural and other incursions, the town retained traces of its indigenous customs generously interwoven with Eurocentric and Christian religious artifacts.

3.5 East and Southern Africa

This region, like other parts of Africa, is no stranger to kingdoms, empires, and urbanization. Foremost among the region's kingdoms are the following: Buganda, which is roughly contemporary Uganda; Rwanda, which thrived around the Lake Nyasa (also known as Lake Victoria) area, the Great Zimbabwe Empire, which covers the territory that the British colonized as Southern Rhodesia; Zulu, which is well-known for its powerful leader, Shaka; the Swazi Kingdom, which exist to date but better known for one of its original leaders, Shubhuza; Sotho Kingdom; and the Ndebele Kingdom. Of these, the Buganda and Great Zimbabwe kingdoms have the most extensive urban experience.

The Ancient Kingdom of Buganda. Founded in the late 13th century, this was one of many small kingdoms established by Bantu-speaking peoples in the general region of what evolved to become Uganda. The first king and founder of the Kintu Dynasty, Kato Kintu, built a powerful military and employed it to expand his territorial influence. In particular, he used all means necessary to subsume his less powerful neighbors under his suzerainty. Initially, the kingdom was led by a king *(or kabaka)* of the Ganda people who instituted a highly centralized vassal state. The state rapidly amassed power and became the dominant kingdom in the region by the 18th and 19th centuries.

The kingdom has a vast urban experience that dates to its founding. It comprised many towns of considerable sizes; prominent in this regard is Lubaga, which was the kingdom's capital. Writing in 1875, the Welsh-American explorer/journalist-cum-colonial-administrator, Henry Morton Stanley described the town as a spatially well-organized human settlement that encircled the royal palace perched atop a hill. The palace itself, Stanley continued, was made up of grass-roofed buildings, including meeting halls and storage buildings, all of which formed a compound enclosed within a tall cane fence. The town was busy and characterized by the same type of dynamics one would find in national capital cities today – the residences of foreign government representatives, ambassadors seeking audiences, messengers and courier services, and law enforcement units.

The Ancient Kingdom of Zimbabwe. Founded in 1220 and thrived until 1450, the Kingdom of Zimbabwe was one of the great empires of ancient Africa. As described in a lucid article in *National Geographic* (2023), it was part of a wealthy African trading empire with dominion over much of the East African coast. The seat of this kingdom's government was Great Zimbabwe, which as portrayed by its ruins, was a large medieval city enclosed by a thick and meticulously constructed mortarless stone wall. Archaeological evidence portrays the city as including a royal palace enclosed within a stone wall and containing several buildings that housed consultants, royals and their offices. The city's inhabitants fell into two main categories, namely those living at the periphery, and those within the core. This latter category was further spatially divided into two groups, including the ruling class and the rest of the city's residents. Members of the ruling class were separated by a thick stone wall from other residents. This suggests that socio-economic spatial segregation predated the European colonial era in Africa.

3.6 Ancient Towns of Foreign Origins

Most of the ancient cities of foreign origins in Africa were established by Europeans. Thus, the presence of Europeans in Africa predates the formal onset of the European colonial era on the continent by at least four centuries. Ironically, the Portuguese, who were only minor players in the colonial project, were the first, and for more than a century, the only Europeans to erect permanent settlements in the form of trading posts on the continent (World Geography, 2023). They built their first trading post in Cape Verde in 1462; thereafter, they constructed a fort on the Gold Coast (present-day Ghana) in 1482. It was not until the 1600s that other Europeans, including the Dutch, the British, the Danes, and the French moved to set up trading posts and forts of their own on the continent. Most European fort- and trading-post-construction initiatives were initially concentrated in West Africa.

One distinguishing feature of the region was the extent to which it had been divided among Europeans of different nationalities. The French, reputed for their commercial orientation, positioned their shops along the Senegal and Gambia rivers. On their part, the British, Danish, and Dutch chose to set up their shops or trading posts on the coast of what evolved to become the nations of Sierra Leone and Ghana. These Europeans are credited with building most of the forts on the West African coasts. Although they counted among the earliest Europeans on the coasts of Africa, the Portuguese built very few forts in the region.

The forts were created along the coasts of the Atlantic and Indian Ocean coasts. Furthest north on the Atlantic coast is Fort St. Louis, which the French created in 1569 as their first trading post in Africa. The fort and its ancillary facilities evolved to form the nucleus of a socio-economically and culturally vibrant city, St. Louis. Located at the mouth of River Senegal, some 320 kilometers (200 miles) in the northwestern region of present-day Senegal, this city played a crucial role in France's escapades in precolonial and colonial Africa. It was the capital of the French colony of Senegal (1673–1902), and the capital of French West Africa (1895–1902). At some point during the colonial era (1920–1957), St. Louis served as the capital of the neighboring French colony Mauritania.

Although the early French inhabitants of St. Louis took no formal steps to promote urbanization, their mere presence significantly contributed to transforming the lifestyles of the city's indigenous residents. As I noted elsewhere, the twilight of France's precolonial presence in Africa coincided with the demise of the slave trade in the French Empire in 1848; it also coincided with the economic transformation that propelled the Industrial Revolution (Njoh, 2022). Among other things, this heightened the importance of agricultural and other raw materials for France's industrial complex.

Consequently, France moved to actively promote large-scale cash-crop farming. This resulted in encouraging capitalist enterprises at the expense of indigenous kinship-based small farming units that employed family labor. Several French merchants, some of whom were already based in St. Louis, proceeded to create agro-industrial enterprises in the Senegal Valley, Thiès and Sine-Saloum regions. This contributed to significant rural-to-urban migration as people previously engaged in small-scale, kinship-based farming moved to seek employment in large-scale agricultural estates.

Southeastward from St. Louis on Gorée Island, one finds two structures, the *maison d'Esclaves*, and the *Fort d'Estrées*. These facilities, a house of slaves and a fortress, as their names suggest, played important roles during the Trans-Atlantic slave trade. The island significantly influenced the growth of Dakar, which is just a little more than a kilometer away. Dakar evolved to replace St. Louis as Senegal's capital city in 1902. Gorée Island, with its two major attractions, the *maison d'Esclaves*, and the *Fort d'Estrées*, continues to make a significant contribution to Dakar's economy and international notoriety as a favorite destination for tourists.

Southeast along the Atlantic coast are Freetown and Monrovia in contemporary Sierra Leone and Liberia, respectively. These are unique because they were never intended as European trading posts. Rather, they were created to serve as permanent settlements for freed enslaved Africans. Freetown was founded as a permanent settlement for freed enslaved Africans from England, United Kingdom under the auspices of the Committee for the Relief of the Black Poor. The first freed slaves settled there in 1887 but were greeted with hostility from members of the indigenous population. With time, the hostile atmosphere intensified, and in 1789, members of the indigenous population burnt to ashes the entire settlement. It was not until 1792 that the settlement was rebuilt. Thereafter, Freetown blossomed and rapidly became, and has since remained, the largest city in Sierra; it is also the country's national capital. Yet, throughout the city's life, there have always been varying degrees of tension between those who see themselves as members of the indigenous population and those who trace their ancestry to freed slaves from England.

Similar tensions constitute a defining feature of life in Monrovia, the capital city of Liberia, Sierra Leone's neighbor to the east. Monrovia, which is located at a place members of the indigenous population called Ducor, was founded in 1822; it was designated a permanent settlement for US-born freed slaves (Dennis, 2006). Named after the US president of the time, James Monroe, the city speedily grew to dwarf the fishing communities within its vicinity around Cape Mesurado and the mouth of the Mesurado River. Soon thereafter, it rose to politically, economically, socially, and culturally surpass all human settlements in the country. It remains Liberia's largest city; it is also the country's administrative and economic capital.

Further eastward along the Atlantic coast from Liberia are Ghana and Ivory Coast, both countries with precolonial towns and cities that owe their growth to European trading posts and cognate facilities. In Ivory Coast, there is Grand Bassam, which served briefly as the French colonial capital in the late 19th century. These influenced the emergence and/or expansion of many human settlements in the coastal region of the country. For instance, it is unlikely that Accra, the capital of contemporary Ghana would have attained its precolonial stature without European facilities such as Fort Osu, which was built in 1652, Fort Crevecoeur, which was erected by the Dutch in 1642, and Fort James, which was constructed by the British in 1873. Jamestown was an outgrowth of Fort Crevecœur, which was renamed Fort Ussher in 1649, and Fort St. James, which was initially developed as a trading post for enslaved persons and gold. Over time, Jamestown expanded to become a part of Accra. On its part, Fort Osu, which was later renamed Fort Christiansburgh, after the Danish King Christian V, grew to become a suburb of Accra.

The development and subsequent expansion of Cape Coast, a Ghanaian city of historical significance, was heavily influenced by Cape Coast Castle. This was a military fortification constructed in 1653 by the Swedes although it was later controlled by the British. The City of Cape Coast grew to, like the Cape Coast Castle, play a fundamental role in the trans-Atlantic slave trade. Another Ghanaian coastal city whose growth was influenced by a precolonial European castle is Elmina. Located in the country's central region, Elmina would not have been the dominant city that it was during the precolonial era without Elmina

Castle. This was constructed by the Portuguese in 1482. Like the castle, the town evolved to play a critical role in the Trans-Atlantic slave trade, gold, and other commodities. Finally, there are the twin cities of Sekondi and Takoradi, which are in the country's western region. A significant portion of Sekondi's growth is due to the creation of a fort by the same name. Fort Sekondi was developed by the Dutch in the 17th century. On its part, Takoradi's growth was significantly influenced by Fort Orange, another Dutch project that was completed in 1642.

In the central region of Africa along the Atlantic coast, European forts and castles, albeit relatively few, also significantly influenced precolonial urbanization on the continent. For instance, the expansion of Luanda in Angola was significantly influenced by Fort São Miguel. The fort, which was constructed in 1576, comprised the nucleus around which Luanda grew to become a major administrative and port city in the region. Further south, one finds Cape Town, whose growth was at least indirectly influenced by European precolonial commercial activities in Africa. Cape Town, it would be recalled, developed as a supply station for the Dutch East India Company's ships en route to the East Indies. This required strong military defense; hence, the creation of the Castle of Good Hope in 1666. This latter became the nucleus around which Cape Town developed and grew to constitute a vital port city and legislative capital of South Africa.

Although Europeans were relatively less involved in trading along the Indian Ocean Coast of Africa, this coast was certainly not without its own share of European forts and trading posts. The few Europeans who managed to create forts and cognate facilities in the region include the British, Dutch, and Portuguese. Although some degree of trading occurred at these fortified facilities, they were mainly designed to serve defense purposes. Some of the facilities are noteworthy because they significantly influenced the creation of new towns or the expansion of existing ones. Counting among the most notable in this regard are, Fort Jesus, Zanzibar and Fort Jesus, Kilwa-Kisiwani in Tanzania and Fort Jesus, Mombasa in Kenya.

Fort Jesus, Zanzibar was built by the Portuguese in the late 16th century; it is located on the Zanzibar Island in present-day Tanzania. At the time of its construction, the island was sparsely inhabited by members of the indigenous population. Subsequently, and thanks at least in part to the fort, the island's population grew, and led to the emergence of a human settlement named Stone Town. Before long, the town had grown and intensified its role as a viable participant in the Indian Ocean spice trade. Today, Stone Town is one of the most densely populated human settlements in Tanzania; it is designated as a UNESCO World Heritage Site thanks especially to its historical architecture and cultural significance.

The Portuguese also constructed a fort on another island, Kilwa-Kisiwani, off the coast of Tanzania. Also named Fort Jesus, this fort, like the one in Zanzibar, was built in the 16th century to protect Portuguese interests in the region. Over time, it came to significantly influence the growth and commercial viability of Kilwa, which at the time, was a vibrant Swahili city-state.

The Portuguese were also responsible for constructing another fort named Fort Jesus in Mombasa, Kenya. The fort was built in 1593; it served as a permanent fortification on the eastern coast of Africa. Its location in Mombasa was strategic because it accentuated Portugal's visibility in the region. To be sure, Mombasa was not a creation of Europeans or any other foreign entity. Rather, it evolved from a human settlement that was founded by the Swahili dynasty, Mwana Mkisi around 900 CE. It thrived as one of the most important trading hubs connecting the Swahili people to India, Persia, and the Arabic Peninsula. Yet, it is unlikely that the City of Mombasa would have gained the notoriety it did as a regional and international center of commerce during the precolonial era and beyond without Fort Jesus.

3.7 Conclusion

When the Europeans on the mission to colonize Africa arrived the continent in the late 19th century, they found human settlements of varying sizes. Some were created by Africans while others were an outgrowth of facilities such as forts or trading posts that had been developed by Europeans whose presence as traders had predated the colonial era. The European trading posts and other European settlements on the continent typically stood in stark contrast to the indigenous African settlements in terms of their architecture. This was true even in the few cases in which buildings in the European settlements were constructed of local materials such as thatch and compressed earth. Another factor that distinguished these European settlements from the indigenous ones was the daily dynamics. The European settlements usually had a large staff comprised of European and African workers with the latter usually in the majority. These settlements evolved to constitute the nucleus around which some of Africa's largest towns developed.

The distinguishing marks of the two types of settlements notwithstanding, there was a lot of interaction, and intermingling between them. At the very basic level, the Europeans were served by Africans from proximate indigenous settlements. And the continuous growth of the population of persons of mixed race – or what was labeled the "mulatto population" was concrete evidence of the intimate relationships that the Europeans, who were almost without exception men, had established with local African women.

4 The Era of Discovery Towns

4.1 Introduction

An important but largely ignored period in the historiography of cities in Africa is the (European) Age of Discovery or Era of Exploration. This period predated the European colonial era, which is the focus of most of the mainstream literature on the continent's urban history. Generally taken to span the period between the 14th and 18th centuries, the Era of European Exploration witnessed the involvement of Europeans in a wide range of activities with implications for human settlement development in Africa. Europeans were particularly involved in masterminding and shepherding the trans-Atlantic slave trade, establishing trading posts and ports, engaging, and interacting with local communities, and promoting Christianity and European technologies. This section discusses these activities with emphasis on their multifaceted effects on urban and regional development throughout the continent. It begins with a panoramic survey of the identified activities, and how they affected human settlement development.

4.2 Age of Discovery Cities in Africa

The trans-Atlantic slave trade was arguably the most dominant activity of Europeans in Africa during the Age of Discovery. Although often ignored by historiographers of cities in Africa, this repugnant trade gave rise to many towns and cities on the continent. Also noteworthy is the extent to which this trade influenced the structures, internal dynamics, state formation, and political organization in these towns (Law, 1991). The following cities, which are discussed in greater detail later, originated as slave markets: Goree Island in Senegal, Elmina in Ghana, Lagos in Nigeria, Ouidah in Benin, Luanda in Angola, and Zanzibar in Tanzania. Apart from directly contributing to building towns such as these, the transatlantic slave trade profoundly affected regional development as it disrupted local economies and societies. For instance, coastal regions that were involved in the trade often experienced population displacement, social upheaval, and economic exploitation.

The Age of Discovery also witnessed the creation of trading posts and forts by Europeans throughout many parts of Africa. As discussed below, these were typically developed along the coasts and were designed to facilitate trade and protect European commercial interests. Some of the settlements that emerged from the posts and forts have since evolved to become large cities such as Cape Town, South Africa and in some cases, megacities such as Lagos in Nigeria. The European traders and explorers who occupied the trading posts and forts unavoidably interacted with Africans in neighboring indigenous communities, establishing diplomatic relations and trading alliances. These interactions invariably facilitated cultural exchanges and influenced the socio-economic dynamics of local communities.

An important activity of the Europeans of this era was the promotion of Christianity. Accordingly, European traders in Africa were often accompanied by Christian missionaries. These were quick to establish missions and build churches mainly, but not exclusively, along the coast. By so doing, they played a significant role in urban development as they established schools, hospitals, and other social facilities. Missionary settlements often evolved to become large urban centers, contributing to the spread of European culture and especially, Christianity. At least five such urban centers come to mind, including Blantyre in Malawi, Lusaka in Zambia, Entebbe in Uganda, Moshi in Tanzania, and Maseru in Lesotho.

Blantyre is one of Malawi's largest cities. Established by the Scottish missionary, David Livingstone in 1859, it originated as a mission station of the Church of Scotland. Its growth was later spurred by its strategic location as a trade center and administrative hub. Some of the cities, such as Lusaka, Entebbe, Moshi, and Maseru, while not created during the Age of Exploration, are noteworthy because of their origin as mission stations early in the colonial era. Lusaka, Zambia's capital, and largest city also originated as a mission station. It was established by European missionaries of the London Missionary Society in the early 20th century. It was later designated the seat of the Government of Northern Rhodesia (contemporary Zambia) in 1935. Entebbe, which is located on the shores of Lake Victoria, was established as a missionary settlement by the Anglican missionaries in the late 19th century. It served as a base for missionary activities and later developed into an administrative and commercial center. Moshi is located near Mount Kilimanjaro in present-day Tanzania. It originated as a German Lutheran mission station in what was then Tanganyika in the late 19th century. It evolved to become a town and is presently a center for coffee production and tourism, serving as a gateway to the Kilimanjaro National Park. Maseru originated as a British missionary outpost in present-day Lesotho. It was established by the Paris Evangelical Missionary Society in the early 19th century and developed into a major urban center and administrative capital of Lesotho.

No discussion of the Era Discovery in Africa can be deemed complete unless it acknowledges the era's role in introducing European technologies and infrastructure on the continent. The first wave of European technology and other artifacts, including firearms, textiles, tools, and crops were introduced on the continent during this period. The period also witnessed European interventions in infrastructure development and administration. These facilitated the growth of urban centers and contributed to the expansion of regional trade networks. However, one would be remiss by failing to draw attention to the negative implications of these developments. These included but were not limited to exploitation, cultural disruption, and social inequality.

4.3 Towns of the Age of Discovery in Africa

Ironically, the Portuguese, who were only minor players in the colonial project, dominated Africa during the Era of Exploration. For a while during that period, they were the only Europeans who had erected permanent settlements in the form of trading posts on the continent (World Geography, 2023). They built their first trading post in Cape Verde in 1462; thereafter, they constructed a fort on the Gold Coast (present-day Ghana) in 1482. It was not until the 1600s that other Europeans, including the Dutch, the British, the Danes, and the French moved to set up trading posts and forts of their own on the continent. Most European fort- and trading-post-construction initiatives were initially concentrated in West Africa.

As stated in Chapter 3, Europeans were quick to divide most of coastal Africa among themselves. Thus, rather early during the European struggle for Africa, the region already appeared to be distinctly divided among European countries. In this regard, the trading companies that represented the French occupied and built trading posts in the general area of the Senegal and Gambia rivers. Trading companies of British, Dutch, and Danish origin were firmly in control of and had constructed trading posts on, the coasts of present-day Sierra Leone, and Ghana. The activities of the British, the Dutch, and the Danes in Ghana were especially heightened. Together, they had constructed as many as twenty-three forts and trading posts in this country alone by 1700. As the trade in enslaved persons grew more intense, Europeans, especially the English, Portuguese, and Dutch extended their efforts to construct trading posts and forts eastward to locales as far away as Luanda in contemporary Angola. These and related facilities that Europeans developed in Africa during the Age of Discovery and way before the formal onset of the European colonial era cannot be ignored in any meaningful discussion of the continent's urban history. This is because many of these, particularly the forts, formed the nucleus around which a significant number of the continent's towns and cities developed.

Table 1 shows the most prominent of the forts, castles, and other facilities that Europeans and people of European origin developed at that time. It also shows the earliest European human settlements, most of which owe their origin or expansion to the European pioneer traders in the region. Recall as discussed in Chapter 3 that the some of the earliest of these settlements were constructed as far back as 1569. Among these were forts and castles such as Elmina and the French trading posts at St. Louis. Later, and particularly post-colonial urban growth in the region radiated from these facilities and commensurate human settlements.

Table 1 European Trading Posts and Resultant Towns in Africa

Item	Town/Castle/Fort	European creator	Year created	Influenced town	Country	Remarks
01.	Fort James	British	1673	Jamestown (Today, part of the Accra).	Ghana	Created as a trading post for gold and enslaved persons.
02.	Fort Osu (Renamed Ft. Christiansburgh)	Swedish	1652	Osu (Today, a suburb of Accra).	Ghana	Renamed Christianburgh after King Christian V by the Danish in 1663. The Danish owned the fort for 200 years, made it the capital of Danish Gold Coast.
03.	Fort Crèvecœur (Renamed Ussher Fort)	Dutch	1642 (expanded in 1649)	Jamestown Today, part of the Accra).	Ghana	Originally, a factory located at distance 2 days of trekking from Elmina Castle.
04.	Fort Sao Miguel	Portuguese	1576	Luanda	Angola	Constructed by Paulo Dias de Novais. It was literally a self-contained town enclosed within a thick

Table 1 (cont.)

Item	Town/Castle/Fort	European creator	Year created	Influenced town	Country	Remarks
						surrounding wall. Served as a trading post from where slaves were exported to Brazil. In 1627, it was designated capital of the Portuguese-owned territory that evolved to become Angola.
05.	Maison des Esclaves (House of Slaves)	French	1776	Gorée Island, Dakar	Senegal	Control of Gorée Island, which was the largest European trading post for slave trade at the time, changed hands from the Portuguese to the Dutch, to the British and then, to the French. The island contained the dungeon for holding slaves and

No.	Name	Builder	Date	Location	Country	Description
						residential facilities for slave traders and workers from the indigenous populations.
06.	Fort d'Estrées	Portuguese	1852	Gorée Island, Dakar.	Senegal	The Portuguese built it to serve as a naval base in the 1850s.
07.	Old Fort of Zanzibar (also known as Ngome Kongwe)	Portuguese	1690s	Stone Town	Tanzania	The Old Fort is the oldest building in Stone Town. It was built as a Portuguese trading post in Zanzibar on the Indian Ocean coast. Stone Town literally grew around the fort.
08.	Fort Jesus	Portuguese	1593–96	Mombasa	Kenya	Designed to serve the military and commercial goals of the Portuguese in the Indian Ocean, which was until then dominated by the East. It is spread over an area of 2.36 Ha. It significantly

Table 1 (cont.)

Item	Town/Castle/Fort	European creator	Year created	Influenced town	Country	Remarks
						impacted the demographic and physical expansion of Mombasa of which it was a part.
09.	Freetown	British	1787	Freetown	Sierra Leone	The British created Freetown as a home for freed enslaved Africans who were based in Britain as domestic slaves during the heydays of the Trans-Atlantic Slave Trade.
10.	Fort Saint Louis	French	1659	Saint Louis	Senegal	Fort St. Louis was the first trading post set up by the French in Africa. The post evolved to become the nucleus around which the one-time capital of French West Africa grew.

11.	Castle of Good Hope	Dutch	1666	Cape Town	South Africa	The Castle of Good Hope was built by the Dutch to serve as replenishment station for voyagers passing through the Cape. It then became then significantly influenced the growth of Cape Town.
12.	Town of Monrovia	Americans	1822	Monrovia	Liberai	Created by the American Colonization Society for freed enslaved people from the U.S.

Source: Compiled by the author.

Consequently, France moved to actively promote large-scale cash-crop farming. This resulted in encouraging capitalist enterprises at the expense of indigenous kinship-based small farming units that employed family labor. Several French merchants, some of whom were already based in St. Louis, proceeded to create agro-industrial enterprises in the Senegal Valley, Thiès, and Sine-Saloum regions. This contributed to significant rural-to-urban migration as people previously engaged in small-scale, kinship-based farming moved to seek employment in large-scale agricultural estates.

Goree Island, which lies southward of St. Louis, was established during the Era of Discovery as a major slave trading center. It served as a gathering point where enslaved Africans were held before embarking on their transatlantic voyage to the Americas. Today, the island and its ancient slave-holding facilities serve as touristic sites. Two of the facilities standout. These are the *maison d'Esclaves*, and the *Fort d'Estrées*. The facilities, which housed slaves and a fortress, also played instrumental roles in the infamous European project to enslave Africans. Their project's role in influencing the growth of human settlements such as Dakar in the region cannot be overstated. It is no exaggeration that Dakar would never have attained its status as the most impactful city in the region without the slave trade. Note that while Dakar did not serve as a slave depot, it was only about one kilometer from Goree Island, the last and arguably most notorious slave depot in West Africa. Also note that Dakar evolved to assume very important roles within the politico-administrative space of French imperialism in Africa. Here, I hasten to note that in 1902 the French imperial government relocated the politico-administrative capital of Senegal from St. Louis to Dakar. This did a lot not only to accentuate Dakar's importance but also accelerate its physical, social and economic development.

Along the Atlantic coast in West Africa we find Freetown and Monrovia in contemporary Sierra Leone and Liberia, respectively. These are unique because they were never intended as European trading posts. Rather, they were created to serve as permanent settlements for freed enslaved Africans. Freetown was founded as a permanent settlement for freed enslaved Africans from England, United Kingdom under the auspices of the Committee for the Relief of the Black Poor. The first freed slaves settled there in 1787 but were greeted with hostility from members of the indigenous population. With time, the hostile atmosphere intensified, and in 1789, members of the indigenous population burnt the entire settlement to ashes. It was not until 1792 that the settlement was rebuilt. Thereafter, Freetown blossomed and rapidly became, and has since remained, the largest city in Sierra; Leone it is also the country's national capital. Throughout the city's history, there have always been varying degrees of tension between those who see themselves as members of the indigenous population and those who trace their ancestry to freed enslaved Africans from England.

4.4 Conclusion

An important but oft-ignored period in the historiography of African cities is the Era of Discovery or the Age of Exploration. Europeans on the continent were preoccupied with the construction of forts, castles, and trading posts. At the same time, they created slave markets, an unforgettable legacy of that era. The reverberating effects of the era remain evident in the cultural, social, and economic landscapes of the continent. The era also witnessed the establishment of several missionary stations, forts, castles, and trading posts, which evolved to become large cities. Hence, it is arguable that Africa continues to experience the effect of human settlements that were created several centuries ago during the Era of Discovery. Therefore, the importance of such settlements for the discourse on contemporary African cities cannot be overstated.

5 Colonial Cities

5.1 Introduction

The "planting and planning" of towns, to borrow the words of the eminent urban historian, Robert Home, was at the heart of the European colonial project in Africa. The British, for instance, employed town formation, Home (1997) wrote, as a strategy to expand and control its colonies. To be sure, as a colonial power of the 19th/20th century, Britain was not alone in this regard. Rather, all colonial powers in Africa, including France, Spain, Portugal, and Germany were, albeit to different degrees, actively involved in human settlement formation efforts. The cities that resulted from these efforts are classified as colonial cities and constitute the focus of this section.

Many features set colonial cities apart from other human settlements in Africa. For one thing, they were typically set up to serve as the seat of colonial national or subnational governments. Thus, colonial cities were usually centers of government administration. For another thing, their core, or the nucleus around which they developed, was modeled on modernist town planning principles. These were initially formulated to guide spatial development in Europe as a means of counteracting the negative externalities of the Industrial Revolution. The principles were transplanted verbatim to Africa as a power, domination, and social control tool. Also, modernist town planning principles were deployed to attain the colonial project's acculturation and assimilation objectives. For yet another thing, colonial towns usually stood in stark contrast to other human settlements within their proximate and remote surroundings. This is because they were never built to resemble indigenous African human settlements. Rather, they were designed to mimic towns in the European colonial master nations. Two specific features of colonial cities in Africa distinguished them from their indigenous counterparts. The first was the segregation of land use activities and racial groups. The second was the lifestyle, which was considered part of the modernization process by proponents but drew the ire of social critics, especially literary artists.

For example, in *"Things Fall Apart,"* which was set in Nigeria and written in 1958 – three years before Nigeria's independence – Chinua Achebe lambasted the influences of colonialism on Lagos, the country's capital city until 1998. In particular, he delved into the protagonist's experiences in the city and showed how these influences, which were usually showcased as elements of modernity clashed with African indigenous culture and tradition. Several decades later, another prolific Nigerian writer, Chimamanda Ngozi Adichie echoed Achebe's sentiments about life in Lagos. Writing in *"Half of a Yellow Sun,"* which is primarily focused on the Nigerian Civil War (1967–1970), Adichie depicts the bustling city life in Lagos and the struggles of its residents amidst political and social upheavals. Similarly, Tsitsi Dangarembga has very few, if any kind words for colonial cities in her novel, *"Nervous Conditions."* Set in colonial Southern Rhodesia (today, Zimbabwe) the novel vividly paints the picture of a rural girl, Tambudzai, and the intractable difficulties she encountered as she struggled to adjust to city life.

The factors that conspired to render city life less compatible with African indigenous culture and tradition were a product of colonial town planning policies. This section discusses the most prominent of these policies including their avowed and covert objectives. It shows how the policies constituted a tool to attain the following objectives of colonialism: acculturation and assimilation of racial others, articulation of colonial government power in conquered territories, guaranteeing of access to scarce resources for preferred groups, perpetuation of the ideology of perceived White racial superiority.

5.2 Europeans and the Planting of Cities in Africa

The formal onset of the European colonial era in Africa was 1884/85; this is when European colonial powers met at the Berlin Conference and agreed to partition the continent among themselves. Before then, and particularly during the Era of Discovery, each of the powers had already staked out claims over specific territories throughout the continent. In many cases, the colonial powers converted facilities or settlements they had earlier set up to serve precolonial purposes into colonial capitals. Elsewhere (see Njoh, 2016), I have discussed France's preoccupation with the creation of capital cities as a means of ascertaining territorial control in Africa. In Senegal, France converted Saint Louis, its first trading post in Tropical Africa, into the capital of French West Africa in

1895. In 1902, this capital was relocated to Dakar, a city whose growth had been significantly influenced by Gorée Island. The French had established this as a holding bay for enslaved persons bound for the Americas. Dakar doubled as the capital of Senegal and French West Africa from 1902 to the end of the colonial era in the region in 1960.

Abidjan was never created to serve as the capital city of French colonial Ivory Coast. Rather, it was founded as a trading post and only retrofitted to assume the role of colonial capital later in its evolution. The French colonial authorities initially designated Grand-Bassam as the capital of colonial Ivory Coast. Grand-Bassam served in this capacity from 1893 until 1900 when Bingerville became the capital. It was not until 1933 that French colonial authorities replaced Bingerville with Abidjan as the colonial capital, a role it served until the end of the colonial era in the country in 1960. Abidjan has since remained the country's postcolonial capital. Brazzaville, Congo (PRC), was created by the French in 1880 to serve as a military post in French Equatorial Africa (FEA). France moved to designate the town the colonial capital of Congo (PRC) upon the official onset of the European colonial era on the continent in 1885, and also the seat of government for FEA in 1910. Libreville, which was initially established to serve as a settlement for freed enslaved Africans from the Americas in 1849, was designated the administrative capital of colonial Gabon.

The British were equally preoccupied with efforts to control the territories they had procured in Africa with the building of colonial government capitals. For instance, they designated Accra, which the Portuguese had established as a trading post in the 15th century the seat of the British colonial government of the Gold Coast-cum-Ghana.

In Sierra Leone, the British designated Freetown, which they had created in 1887 to serve as a settlement for freed enslaved Africans, the country's administrative capital. Cape Town was created by the Dutch East India Company in 1652 to serve as a refreshment and replenishing station for voyagers bound for the East Indies; it was designated the capital of the Cape Colony during the Dutch/British colonial eras.

A copious entry in Encyclopedia Almanacs (2023) describes how the creation of the Cape Colony amounted to sowing the seed of a regional urban heritage in southern Africa. Similar to a process that had occurred earlier on in Zanzibar, the Cape colony's towns soon developed an international flavor of their own. It did not take long before Cape, the colony's capital, had gained a reputation for housing a mix of sailors and other ship workers from all over the world, slaves from India and Indonesia as well as Dutch, French Huguenots and members of Khoi and San African communities. They lived either as free people or visitors of resident Boer families. In Angola, the Portuguese designated Luanda, which they had founded in 1575 the colonized territory's capital. It was retained as the national capital when the country became independent in 1975.

In some cases, colonial powers simply appropriated towns that had been created by indigenous authorities, modified and designated them as colonial capitals. Two examples, Buea in Cameroon, and Tananarive, Madagascar come to mind. Buea, which served as the capital of German colonial Kamerun (1884–1916), was a small town created by the Bakweri people on the slopes of Mount Cameroon when the German colonial era began in Cameroon in 1884. Upon designating it as the colonial capital, the Germans began modifying the town. These modifications included the construction of colonial government facilities such as the Governor's Mansion, offices, and residential units for colonial functionaries, streets, and utility infrastructure. At about the same time, French colonial authorities in Madagascar were modifying Tananarive (later renamed, Antananarivo) to assume a new role as the seat of French colonial Madagascar's government. Before that time, Tananarive, which had been created in the 17th century by the indigenous Merina Kingdom, was just another indigenous human settlement.

Many of the cities were established as seats of colonial governments after the formal onset of the European colonial era on the continent. Counting among these are Conakry, Guinea; Nairobi, Kenya; Kampala, Uganda; Lusaka, Zambia; Dar-es-Salaam, Tanzania; Windhoek, Namibia; Harare, Zimbabwe; and Maputo, Mozambique. As Encyclopedia Almanacs (2023) articulated, while these began as small colonial administrative centers, because of their designation as seats of colonial governments, they eventually grew into large human settlements. However, the rate of urbanization was never uniform across the board; rather, it differed from one colony to the next, particularly between settler and nonsettler colonies. In settler colonies, that is, mainly southern and eastern Africa, the rate of urbanization was accelerated thanks to the rapid population increase occasioned by the discovery of gold and diamonds in the mid to late 19th century. This discovery led to the creation of cities such as Johannesburg and the expansion of existing human settlements in the region. The discovery complicated South Africa's race relations problem of the time especially in urban areas. Major cities in the country increasingly attracted Europeans, Asians, and people from other African countries. African farmers and herders from different parts of South Africa also flocked to the cities in droves as their rural lands were being appropriated by White settlers with the acquiescence of the state. The rapidly increasing populations in the cities were viewed by city officials and the South African state writ large as a cause for consternation. This led to the enactment of pieces of legislation such as the infamous pass laws that restricted the presence of Blacks in certain cities and the creation of separate exclusively Black townships.

In other parts of Africa, conferring the status of colonial government administrative center on a town remained a leading propellant of urbanization. In West Africa, for instance, Conakry, which originated as a small fishing village experienced rapid growth once it was designated colonial Guinea's capital in 1887. It was retained as the capital city when the country became independent in 1958. Nairobi initially served as a British colonial railway depot in 1899 when the Kenya-Uganda Railway was being constructed. In 1907, the town was designated the seat of the colonial government of British Each Africa. Kampala, which was founded by the British colonial government in 1890 to serve as a military outpost was designated the capital of colonial Uganda that same year. It later developed into a major commercial and colonial government city. Salisbury, which was later renamed Harare, was founded by the British colonial government and designated the seat of the government of colonial Southern Rhodesia (present-day Zimbabwe) in 1890.

By designating Dar es Salaam the administrative capital of Tanganyika in the 19th century, the Germans accelerated the town's urbanization process. The town continued on its rapid growth path when it was retained as the postcolonial capital of the Federal Republic of Tanzania. This combined the erstwhile colonies of Tanganyika and Zanzibar. Lusaka was created by British colonial authorities to serve as the administrative capital for the colonial government of Northern Rhodesia in 1905. The colonial territory later became independent as Zambia and retained Lusaka as its capital. Initially founded by the Portuguese in the late 18th century, Lourenço Marques was designated the colonial capital of Portuguese East Africa in 1898. Lourenço Marques was renamed Maputo and retained as the capital of the colony which became Mozambique at independence in 1975.

Lomé, Togo and Windhoek, Namibia, are two towns that were designated colonial capitals by the Germans at the official onset of the European colonial era in Africa. The Germans extended protectorate status to Togoland in 1884. However, it was not until 1897 that Lomé, which had been a German trading post on the West African coast since 1882 was designated the seat of colonial Togoland. Thereafter, Lomé experienced tremendous growth and remains the capital of, and largest city in, postcolonial Togo. In their South-West Africa colony of Namibia, the Germans designated Windhoek as the administrative capital in 1890. Since then, the city has experienced significant demographic and spatial growth and remains the seat of independent Namibia's government.

5.3 Colonial Commercial Capital Cities

Conferring a city with the status of commercial capital was always guaranteed to influence the growth trajectory of the city. In most cases, for example, Dakar, Freetown, Lomé, Lagos, Libreville, Luanda, and Maputo, the colonial administrative capital was also the colony's modern commercial hub. One of the few exceptions is the port city of Douala, which was the commercial hub but not the administrative capital of German colonial Kamerun. Before establishing colonial control over the territory in 1884, Douala was a small town comprising mainly members of the indigenous population who indulged in fishing.

Cognizant of its strategic importance for their efforts to tap and export essential resources such as timber, rubber, banana, ivory, and palm oil from the territory, German colonial authorities embarked on an ambitious program to develop the port. The program was not exclusively focused on the port; rather it included the construction of roads and railways that linked the port to hinterland locales in the territory. To take further advantage of the commercial value of the port, German colonial authorities enlisted the involvement of German trading companies and merchants. These were active in facilitating trade, creating commercial networks, and deriving profits from the exploitation of the territory's natural resources. Before long, Douala had become the destination of choice for job seekers from neighboring towns and distant locales. Thus, by developing the Douala port as part of their colonial project in Kamerun, the Germans effectively transformed a previously small fishing town into a large commercial city. It has remained postcolonial Cameroon's most populous city for more than a century since the Germans relinquished control over the country in 1919.

The demographic and physical growth of Douala was already visible early in the German colonial era. At the time, specific neighborhoods in the city were already being noticed for the growing population of immigrants from the hinterlands, and neighboring countries. At the same time, the European population was also experiencing a surge. It did not take long for certain neighborhoods in the city, especially Akwa, New Bell, Bonaberi, and Akwa-Nord to be reputed as immigrant enclaves. These neighborhoods were instrumental in shaping colonial Douala's social, cultural, economic, and political landscape. Above all, the presence of immigrants from diverse backgrounds enriched the city's cultural fabric and played a formidable role in making it a veritably multicultural, cosmopolitan, and dynamic urban center.

5.4 Colonial Cities, Replicas of European Human Settlements

The story of the planning and planting of colonial towns in Africa is virtually incomplete without mention of the extent to which colonial authorities went to create replicas of European towns in Africa. The objective was to impose Eurocentric architectural and spatial planning ideals on colonial cities to create familiar and recognizable built environments that bear a striking resemblance to their home countries. Five of the continent's major cities, Brazzaville, Congo PR; Dakar, Senegal; Maputo, Mozambique; Nairobi, Kenya; and Kinshasa, Congo DR come to mind in this connection.

Brazzaville, the seat of the government of the present-day People's Republic of Congo, was, as mentioned earlier, the capital of French Equatorial Africa (1910–1958). To afford it an image befitting of the seat of a federation's government, colonial urban planners designed it in conformity with French notions of beauty and aesthetics. Accordingly, the city plan came complete with tree-lined boulevards, huge public buildings, and squares adhering to the dictates of Haussmannian architecture (named after Georges-Eugène Haussmann, prefect of Seine from 1853 to 1870). Budgetary constraints inhibited the complete realization of this plan. Nevertheless, Brazzaville of the immediate postcolonial era bore at least a passing resemblance to 19th-century Paris whose design was also influenced by Haussmannian design principles. The design of Dakar, the capital of contemporary Senegal, was also heavily influenced by Haussmannian design principles. In this regard, the city was designed to incorporate wide streets, French-style grand buildings, and a generous supply of green spaces and public squares.

Kinshasa, which was known as Léopoldville during the colonial era was the capital of Belgian Congo and has since remained the capital of the independent Democratic Republic of Congo. Its design was heavily influenced by European, particularly Belgian concepts of spatial organization. The design called for the incorporation of wide boulevards, neoclassical physical structures, and parks that afford it a striking resemblance to vintage European cities, particularly Brussels.

Maputo, which was known as Lourenço Marques during the colonial era, was designed to embody European and particularly Portuguese architectural styles. As the capital of Portuguese East Africa (today, Mozambique), the city's design came complete with wide streets or boulevards flanked by large imposing public buildings and many public squares and green spaces. This conformed with vintage Portuguese colonial urban architecture.

Nairobi served as the capital of British East Africa. The British created this as a protectorate in 1895 and designated Mombasa its capital. In 1905, the capital was relocated to Nairobi, which was retained as the capital of colonial Kenya, and later as the country's postcolonial capital. Although Nairobi was never designed to mimic any specific British or European city, the grid-iron pattern incorporated in its design structure gives it a vintage British look. Although colonial cities were designed to serve as administrative centers, their contribution to the colonial project transcended this immediate objective. These cities stood as symbols of European domination, power, and social control in colonial Africa.

An assertion in the Encyclopedia Almanacs (2023) to the effect that colonialism fostered socio-economic growth and spatial expansion in Africa is bolstered by much evidence. The act of designating a town as a colonial capital was always accompanied by the construction in that town of streets and other transportation infrastructure, government buildings, administrative centers, healthcare centers, schools, and commensurate facilities. These were all necessary to facilitate colonial government functioning. The facilities also had the unintended effect of attracting people from other parts of the colony and the wider region of which it was a part. This explains the fact that, almost without exception, all cities that originated as colonial administrative centers throughout Africa evolved rather speedily to assume roles such as the melting pot of various ethnicities, cultures, and languages. In many cases, such as those of Dakar in Senegal, Abidjan in Côte d'Ivoire, Accra in Ghana, Cotonou in Benin, Freetown in Sierra Leone, Lagos in Nigeria, Libreville in Gabon, and Luanda, Angola, the cities became the economic hubs of their respective countries. As coastal locales, these cities naturally became centers for exporting agricultural and other products; through this, they invariably contribute to their national economies as they continue to attract immigrants from hinterland locales.

Efforts to mimic European concepts and ideals of spatial organization attained their zenith in schemes that sought to adhere to the garden city principles of Ebenezer Howard. Many European colonial initiatives to plan and plant cities in Africa were dedicated to incorporating these principles, which are essentially designed to enhance the quality of life for urban dwellers. In practice, this called for the inclusion of urban planning features such as spacious residential areas, green spaces, greenbelts, and a functional system of streets and pedestrian walkways. Many cities in Africa, or at least their blueprints, contain garden city features. Foremost among these cities are Accra, Ghana; Lusaka, Zambia; Nairobi, Kenya; and Pretoria (Tshwane), South Africa.

5.5 Racial Spatial Segregation in Colonial Towns

Racial spatial segregation was a conspicuous feature of the colonial city throughout Africa. This is incontestable! What is, however, debatable is why, despite their respective ideological leanings, European colonial powers without exception adopted racial spatial segregation policies in their African colonies. There were many reasons for this, but the following three are often submitted and appear to be the most persuasive (Njoh, 2008). One of these is the dominant race ideology of the period leading up to the formal onset of the European colonial era in Africa. Propagated by the likes of the English-born American Egyptologist, George Gliddon (1809–1857) and the French sociologist, Arthur Comte de Gobineau (1816–1882), this ideology classified humans on a three-rung ladder. Within this framework, Whites, the so-called "Aryan master race," occupied the top-most rung, while Asians (or "mongoloids") occupied the middle rung, and Africans (and all persons of African descent) were at the lowest rung. In the words of Comte de Gobineau, the racial classification scheme can be summarized thus: "superior Caucasoids," "intermediate Mongoloids," and "inferior Negroids" (Gobineau, 1853/1967). Central to the race ideology was the outright rejection of "race mixing." The policy of racial segregation widely adopted by colonial governments in Africa can, therefore, be seen as a function of the pervasive racialized ideology of the time.

Another oft-submitted reason concerns protecting the health of the European population in Africa. Rather early in the colonial era, it had become evident that malaria was the leading cause of early death among Europeans on the continent. British colonial authorities were particularly perturbed by the mortality rate among European malaria patients; consequently, they commissioned several studies to uncover the problem's roots. The studies were conducted between 1899 and 1900 by researchers at the Liverpool School of Tropical Medicines under the auspices of Dr. Ronald Ross. Data for the studies came from Sierra Leone, which was considered a bastion of the anopheles mosquito at the time. They revealed that the anopheles mosquito, a largely nocturnal insect, was the sole vector of the malaria-causing parasite. It also erroneously pinpointed Africans as the sole intermediate host and reservoir of this parasite. Based on these revelations, the nocturnal separation of Europeans from Africans was mandated. This rationale explains the 1901 decision by Joseph Chamberlain, the British Colonial Secretary at the time, to mandate exclusive European enclaves in Britain's tropical African colonies.

Yet another reason for racial spatial segregation policies in Africa concerns the need to buttress and broadcast the perceived superiority of the White race. Accordingly, segregation policies created privileged enclaves of access that helped Europeans in colonial cities to consolidate the power they wielded over "racial others." These enclaves, which were typically perched atop elevated plateaus ensured that: (1) the best and lion's share of land in colonial cities was occupied by Europeans; and (2) Africans and members of other races such as Asians, were always under the constant gaze of European colonial authorities. This explains the popularity of high altitudes separated by a considerable distance from the town center as the location of choice for government administrative offices and European enclaves writ large in colonial Africa.

These rationales are not mutually exclusive; rather, they overlap. It is therefore no paradox that racially segregated spatial structures were as common in colonial cities controlled by Northern Europeans who were more conscious of race as a distinguishing feature of humans as they were in cities controlled by Southern Europeans who acknowledged culture as the defining feature of humans. Yet, there is no denying that some urban Africans in countries with a history of British, especially settler, colonialism experienced some of the most blatant racial segregation policies. Consider the case of Apartheid South Africa. Here, there were laws designed to keep non-Whites entirely out of cities or at least, restrict their access to same. The country's racial segregation laws such as the Natives Land Act No. 27 of 1913 and the Natives (Urban Areas) Act of 1923 were designed to limit the access of non-Whites to urban and other highly desirable areas. The "Pass Laws," which constituted a critical component of the apartheid system, required Blacks to carry passbooks whenever they were outside the "Black-only" areas or "homelands." As stipulated by the Natives (Abolition of Passes and Co-ordination of Documents) Act of 1952, a passbook contained the bearer's photograph, details of his/her place of origin, employment record, tax payments and information on any encounters with the police. Apartheid laws were most strictly implemented in highly sought-after cities such as Johannesburg, Cape Town and Durban. These cities had exclusive "Whites-Only" neighborhoods and districts.

Kenya and Zimbabwe, which were, to some extent, settler colonies also experienced a heightened level of racial segregation. In colonial Kenya, Nairobi's "racial tripartition" resulted in the entire picturesque north-western areas, which contained the city's most valuable land assigned exclusively to Europeans, while the second-best desirable areas in the city's north-eastern region were designated as exclusive Asian districts. Members of the native population were confined within the small and least desirable area in the eastern and southern quadrant of the city. This racialized spatial distribution schemata resulted in assigning areas such as Karen and Muthaiga, both suburbs of Nairobi, exclusively to Europeans. This was tantamount to creating distinct enclaves with privileged access to the most desirable resources and amenities. The districts are well-known for their spacious residential properties, well-maintained gardens, and exclusive social clubs.

Similarly, in Salisbury (present-day, Harare), Rhodesia (today, Zimbabwe) colonial authorities had developed neighborhoods such as Borrowdale and Highlands as exclusive White enclaves. These offered modern amenities and access to services not available to non-White communities. In his insightful analysis of electricity provisioning in colonial Bulawayo, Moses Chikowero (2007) described how the city's electrification project was racially biased; it benefited exclusively the city's white settler community. The Bulawayo Town Council, he stressed, harnessed electrical energy to exclude Africans spatially from, and to contain them within, certain urban spaces. The council's view of Africans as subhuman and not deserving of the same rights as the city's white settler population led to racially discriminatory policies in other milieus. For example, in 1912–29, the council proceeded to destroy housing units belonging to Africans in Makokoba, an exclusively African residential area. The displaced homeowners lost their ownership rights and were compelled to seek accommodation in the council's substandard cottages where they had no tenancy rights or hopes of ameliorating their living conditions.

The ideological nuances notwithstanding, racial spatial segregation policies succeeded in attaining one specific objective in colonial cities throughout Africa. They compartmentalized built space in a manner that allotted the most desirable and strategically located areas – usually at high altitudes – to Europeans. The converse, within this scheme, was that the least attractive – usually low-lying areas – were assigned to non-Whites, with Africans always occupying the least habitable districts.

The earliest and best-known formal initiative in this connection occurred in Freetown, Sierra Leone. This was the first effort to implement the 1901 policy mandating racially segregated towns in British colonies in tropical Africa. The effort entailed developing an exclusive European enclave on the plateau of a hill overlooking the rest of the City of Freetown. Known as Hill Station, the enclave was connected to Freetown by a narrow gauge, custom-built mountain railway. The choice of a plateau as the locale for an exclusive European enclave was meant to serve more than just health objectives. It was also intended to symbolize power.

Yet, British colonial authorities were not the only ones to appreciate the value of elevated terrain as a symbol of power, hence the ideal locale for exclusive European enclaves in colonial Africa. German colonial authorities are also on record for electing to locate exclusive European enclaves in similar spots. The colonial stations that the Germans developed in 1902 respectively in Bamenda and Buea in Kamerun (today, Cameroon), exemplify this tendency. Not to be outdone, the French also employed altitude to symbolize power by electing to locate exclusive European enclaves on elevated terrain.

Urban historian, Phyllis Martin paints a lucid picture of how French colonial authorities in Brazzaville employed elevation, and topography writ large to symbolize power. The year was 1909, and French colonial authorities in Brazzaville, the capital of French Equatorial Africa, had just received the mandate from the metropole to racially segregate the city. In response, they created separate districts for Europeans and Africans. The European district, which included the colonial government station was located on the most elevated plateau in the city. The African district was called Poto Poto, and was in a depressed, swampy, and muddy part of the city. Movement within and beyond the villages was strictly controlled, and the community was permanently under a 9 p.m. curfew as per a law of 1926. Meanwhile, a law of 1904 had earlier banned drumming in the area except during certain hours of the weekend.

In colonial Leopoldville (today, Kinshasa), the Belgians created a 500-meter strip of land between the European enclave and the native district. The two were arranged so that the European enclave would always be on an elevated terrain, and never downwind from the African district. French colonial urban planners manipulated urban space to ensure that European and native districts were separated by swamps (in Pointe Noire) and lagoons (in Abidjan).

In the absence of elevated terrain, the distinction was more linguistic than otherwise. Consider the case of colonial Bamako; here, government buildings and the residences of colonial officials were located on Koulouba, a cliff overlooking the African districts. The same holds for colonial Dakar, Senegal; Abidjan, Cote d'Ivoire; and Libreville Gabon, where the most elevated land in the city was labeled "plateau" and designated exclusive White enclaves. Ironically, even Niamey, Niger, which had no elevated land, had a plateau. Making this observation in 1982, Christopher Winters contended, while the city has no plateau, it nevertheless has a Plateau (Winters, 1982).

5.6 Conclusion

The roots of colonial cities in Africa can be traced to at least three sources. The first is an indigenous African town. This would typically have been an existing city that European colonial authorities simply appropriated for use in discharging one or more colonial government functions. The second is a trading post whose roots may be traceable to the Era of Discovery, and which colonial authorities designated as a colonial government administrative center. The third is a city developed from scratch to serve as the seat of a colonial government. These roots notwithstanding, once designated the seat of a colonial government, the cities became the focus of intense colonial government infrastructure development initiatives. This in turn made the cities the destination of choice for immigrants from all over the country. Once in the city, immigrants tend to congregate in stranger quarters that typically correspond with their hometowns or places of nativity. The stranger quarter phenomenon, discussed in Section 7, is a product of this.

6 Colonial Company Towns

6.1 Introduction

The story of how the European colonial project affected urbanization in Africa remains incomplete without mention of the role of company towns and employer-supplied housing. These typically included ancillary units such as convenience stores, canteens, and recreational facilities. They were usually created by colonial governments, mining companies, plantation agricultural firms, natural resource extraction corporations, and other formal sector entities. These corporations developed company towns to meet the housing and related needs of their employees.

Counting among the prominent company towns of the colonial era were facilities designed to house colonial government employees such as Government Residential Areas (GRAs), and military barracks. These, as noted by Homes (2000), were first introduced in Africa in the 19th century; they signify a period when colonial governments provided housing for their employees and mandated formal private sectors to do likewise. These were, as van der Watt and Maris (2019) described them, the days when formal sector employers made decisions for their employees and provided them with housing and social services. They constituted a central component of the colonial project and were essential in efforts to realize the economic objective of this project. As Robert Home once observed, company towns and employer-supplied housing writ large, constitute "the commonest built element in the colonial landscape" in Africa (2000: 328). Yet, such facilities were never a direct factor of production. Rather, they facilitated the economic exploitation agenda of the project by guaranteeing colonial corporations uninhibited control over an important factor of production, namely labor.

Cognizant of this, colonial authorities prioritized the creation and maintenance of company towns on the colonial development agenda. As used here, the notion of company towns is generic and includes all employer-provided housing facilities. These were commonplace, and in a good number of cases, mandated by law in colonial Africa. Some knowledge of these laws is necessary to better appreciate the contribution of employer-provided housing in the making of the city in Africa. By directly housing their employees, the colonial natural resource extraction corporations and other employers in the colonial theater were guaranteed round-the-clock control over their employees. Company towns or employer-provided housing, generically, affected how and where most formal sector workers in colonial Africa lived. More importantly, these towns, which I have described elsewhere as counting among the indelible imprints of colonialism on Africa's landscape (Njoh, 2007), significantly influenced the course of urbanization on the continent.

6.2 Employer-Provided Housing in Colonial Africa

Most of the company towns, or the ruins thereof, found throughout Africa were created during the heydays of the European colonial era. These towns, and employer-provided housing in general, most of which exist to date, were often mandated by law. Yet, because of their intrinsic advantages, employers were almost always prepared to house their employees even without the laws that required them to do so. Employers in colonial economies derived many advantages from housing their employees. For example, such housing permitted employers to control workers' behavior. Also, such housing served as a conduit for the transmission of Eurocentric concepts of household composition, housing, and spatial organization. This explains, at least partially, the colonial government laws mandating employer-supplied housing. A few examples of these laws, drawn largely from erstwhile British colonies, are illuminating.

In South Africa, there was the Mines and Works Act of 1911 that required mining companies to provide adequate housing for their employees. The avowed aim of the law was to regulate the living conditions of mine workers as well as prevent overcrowding and improve sanitation conditions in mining communities. In Nigeria, the British colonial government enacted a law, the Native Housing Ordinance, in 1913 that mandated employers to provide housing to native African workers in certain industries. Additionally, the law codified standards for housing conditions and established rent control measures designed to prevent rent-hiking by landlords in urban areas. In colonial Kenya, the government enacted a law in 1920, the Native Housing Act, that compelled employers to provide housing to their African workers. The law was designed to specifically address the problem of standard housing shortage that was already exhibiting signs of severity in urban Kenya in the early 20th century.

The British colonial government of Ghana also took action to compel employers to provide adequate housing to their employees. This action was codified by the Labour Ordinance of 1951; the avowed aim of this ordinance was to improve the living conditions of formal sector workers in urban areas. Accordingly, the ordinance established standards for housing construction, the provisioning of amenities, sanitation, and cognate facilities. In Northern Rhodesia (present-day, Zambia), the British colonial government was once more at work taking action to compel formal sector employers to adequately house their employees. This was done through the enactment of the Native Administration Proclamation in 1958.

To be sure, the British were not the only colonial power that enacted laws requiring formal sector employers to provide housing for their employees. The French were also active in this domain. For example, the *Loi Lamine Guèye,* which was enacted in 1946, was designed to fulfill this objective in the Federation of French West Africa; this included present-day Senegal, Mali, Ivory Coast, Niger, Mauritania, Burkina Faso, Chad, and Benin. In French colonial Algeria, it was the *Loi Cadre,* which was enacted in 1956 that played the same role. However, the law went further as it included provisions relating not only to housing but also to labor rights, and workers' conditions in general. On the part of the Portuguese, they had the Colonial Labor Code, which included provisions requiring formal sector employers in Angola, Mozambique and Guinea-Bissau to provide housing to their employees. Labor laws in German colonies such as German East Africa, including Tanganyika (the mainland part of contemporary Tanzania), Rwanda, and Burundi, boasted similar provisions. While the laws were designed to enhance the quality of the housing stock in a bid to improve the living conditions of workers, they were mainly driven by the need to attain certain objectives of the colonial project. One of these relates to the colonial powers' economic interests; it also included the need to actualize the perceived superiority of Whites vis-à-vis "racial others." To attain this latter objective, the layout of these towns was made to strictly maintain racial segregation as a means of fostering inequality between European and African workers.

6.3 Types of Employer-Supplied Housing

Employer-supplied housing came in many forms with the following being fore-most: single-family, line houses, compound housing, hostels, and barracks. Single-family housing was typically provided by companies with ample resources to employees of higher standing. They usually comprised free-standing bungalows or other structures that ranged from simple housing to more comfortable dwellings. Line houses were among the most common types of employer-supplied housing in the agricultural plantation sector in colonial Africa. These were typically rows of connected houses, often positioned along straight lines. Each unit accommodated a single worker or small family.

Line houses provided the bare minimum required of standard housing and were often preferred by plantation companies because of their low cost and ease of construction. Compound housing comprised a cluster of houses, typically config-ured around a courtyard or common area. In a way, they were designed to simulate a typical indigenous African family compound. They were few and far between, and usually housed a small group of workers at a time, and only rarely were they assigned to a single large family. Hostels or dormitory-style housing ranked among the most common employer-supplied housing in the extractive sector, particularly mining, in colonial Africa. They typically assumed the form of large buildings that contained sleeping quarters and shared ancillary facilities, including dining halls, bathrooms, and recreational spaces. Their avowed purpose was to accommodate workers in a centralized location with easy access to their workplaces.

Barracks or barrack-style residential facilities constituted the most common form of employer-supplied housing in colonial Africa. These were like hostels in some cases. However, in most cases, they assumed the form of large buildings subdivided into smaller rooms or compartments, designed to accommodate multiple workers or families. First introduced on the continent by colonial corporations in the extractive industry in the 19th century, barracks were typically basic and utilitarian in design. They offered limited privacy and shared sanitation facilities. This housing option, which had become commonplace, especially as a facility for housing soldiers, was the object of criticism in the mid 19th century. It was linked to the high incidence of communicable diseases and mortality rates among soldiers. Living conditions had become a cause for concern not only in military barracks but in employer-supplied housing writ large.

This prompted the reaction of colonial governments who set up commissions of inquiry to investigate and recommend actions necessary to improve workers' housing. One such commission, the Native Housing Commission was established in South Africa in 1924. It was charged with examining the housing situation, sanitation, and related matters affecting African communities in urban areas. A similar commission, the Indigenous Labor Commission, was set up in Kenya in 1931. Its main task was to, among other things, examine, and recommend improvements to, housing conditions for Africans in urban areas. A year later witnessed the creation of the Witwatersrand Native Labour Association Commission in 1932. This commission was charged with inquiring into the working and living conditions of African miners in the Witwatersrand area. The investigation focused intensely on the conditions of mining workers' housing. All the reports revealed that the conditions of employer-supplied housing left much to be desired.

Notwithstanding, the colonial state throughout Africa continued to promote employer-supplied housing, especially for non-White workers. An important driving force behind this was the fact that most workers in the extractive sector were immigrants from distant and/or hinterland locales. In Cameroon, for instance, workers in coastal rubber, banana, and oil palm plantations were mainly from the grass fields. In Ghana and Ivory Coast, workers in the cocoa plantations were usually from landlocked neighboring countries such as Upper Volta (contemporary, Burkina Faso), Mali, and Niger. In South Africa, mine workers were largely immigrants from hinterland countries such as Bechuanaland (today, Botswana), Southern Rhodesia (today, Zimbabwe), and Northern Rhodesia (contemporary Zambia).

Certainly, corporations in the extractive and agricultural plantation sector were not the only ones who established workers' camps or towns. Rather, companies in other sectors were active in this arena. For instance, in the 1920s, the Abidjan-Niger Railway Company *(Compagnie des Chemins de Fer Abidjan-Niger)*, the French company that constructed railways in colonial Ivory Coast, built camps along the railways to house its employees. Prominent among these is the camp that was built in the city of Bouake, central Ivory Coast. This evolved to become a hub of the railway construction company's activities in the region.

6.4 Company Towns and Rural Urbanization in Africa

From their inception during the colonial era, company towns in Africa have always been built in remote, undeveloped, and unincorporated areas. The resource extraction and agro-industrial corporations that ran these towns operated them as temporary pioneering devices (Porteus, 1970). In this case, the towns were used as a means of initiating development on virgin terrain. Thus, company towns were effectively used to actualize what Lance van Sittert (2001) once characterized as an archetypical urban form on the rural periphery. The need to appreciate this unique instrument of urbanization cannot be overstated. As a lesson in African urban history, company towns afford a rare opportunity to understand rural urbanization and the role the state and capital played in urban development in colonial Africa. Paradoxically, there is no inherent terminological contradiction in the notion of rural urbanization. This is especially true when urbanization is viewed through the lenses of German-born classical Chicago School sociologist, Louis Wirth. Writing in his 1938 classic, "Urbanism as a Way of Life," Wirth underscored the need to view urbanization not only from a quantitative perspective but also in terms of the composition and lifestyles of the human settlements (Wirth, 1938).

Composition as a defining feature of urbanism speaks to the extent to which a human settlement is heterogeneous. Seen from this vantage point, company towns, without exception, were by nature, heterogeneous. Once a company created a workers' camp or company town, it immediately proceeded to assign the units therein to members of its workforce according to their professional ranks. The workers were typically drawn from all nooks and crannies of the colonized territory. Thus, the towns were typically heterogeneous in terms of their resident population. However, because of the need to restrict access to scarce urban goods and services to Whites, the colonial resource extraction companies actively maintained racially segregated spatial structures. It was common for mining companies, for instance, to build company towns exclusively for their White employees, while housing members of their African workforce in single-sex hostels or compounds. It was not until the early 2000s that this latter system was abolished throughout South Africa.

Thus, a prominent feature of company towns was segregation; this was at two levels, racially, and then, along socio-economic lines. As their name suggests, they were usually managed and controlled by the companies that owned them.

Therefore, in each case, the company doubled as a municipal authority, and as the township manager, and landlord. Thus, the companies, which operated mainly in the resource extractive sector, played a significant role in shaping the growth and proliferation of the towns to support their operations. Company towns must, therefore, be seen as vibrant actors in the colonial economic space. They affected urban development or urbanization in general in two ways – directly and indirectly. As additional objects in built space, their impact on the course of urbanization was direct. However, by providing the opportunity for generating and spending income, which in turn contributes to economic growth, the impact of company towns on urbanization is indirect. Yet, company towns and their ancillaries were not, in and of themselves, means of economic production. Rather, they were part of the infrastructure that facilitated such production.

The lifestyle typically associated with urbanization is replete with elements of Eurocentric or Western values and norms encapsulated by the euphemism, modernity. Urbanization is considered synonymous with modernity in Western ethos. This was more so during the colonial era when colonial powers avowed modernization as an important goal of colonization. The planting of company towns in rural areas constituted part of efforts to attain this goal. For colonial authorities, every phase of the company town creation process was an opportunity to promote one or another aspect of European culture. The spatial structure of choice for the towns was the grid-iron pattern, a well-known Eurocentric strategy for ensuring a sense of order and economic efficiency in built space. When it came to erecting the buildings, almost exclusively European building materials were used.

To appreciate the extent to which the planting of company towns helped to advance colonial urbanization efforts in Africa, it helps to reflect on the continent's stage of development in the 19th century. At that time, the continent was almost completely agrarian, and rural living was associated with non-Western societies. In contrast, urbanization was considered an aspect of Western ethos and associated with modernity. Company towns were constructed of European building materials. In the British colonies, for instance, cement came in bags boldly marked "Portland Cement." Portland was not just a trade name. Rather, it was meant to commemorate Portland in Dorset, England. This is the source of the main ingredient that went into the cement when it was first manufactured by the British, Joseph Aspdin in 1824. The cement was used to mold the blocks and produce the concrete used in building company towns in British colonies. The roofing sheets, which were usually of the corrugated variety, were also imported from Europe. Consequently, the company towns with their alien buildings and spatial configuration stood in stark contrast to other structures within the surrounding rural space.

Thus, the mining and agricultural plantation companies also seized the occasion to supply housing to their middle- and upper-income employees as an opportunity to showcase Eurocentric living standards and promote urbanization. Accordingly, they built self-contained housing units, complete with kitchens, internal plumbing, and electrical installations. Among other things, this effectively replaced firewood, a well-known indigenous African cooking and lighting fuel with electricity or natural gas. These efforts were complemented by propaganda and other campaigns such as movie or cinema shows. This, as I noted elsewhere, was a staple of the entertainment diet that an agro-plantation corporation in colonial Anglo-Cameroon fed residents of its company towns (Njoh et al., 2020). The same corporation, as others throughout colonial Africa, also operated schools for the workers' children, and domestic science or home economic classes for their wives. These were designed to instill Eurocentric values and so-called modern ways of doing things in Africans. Furthermore, there were active programs to use workers' housing facilities as an instrument for instituting Eurocentric concepts of leisure and time management in Africa. It is in this context that the provisioning of golf courses, football fields, tennis courts, and other recreational facilities found in many company towns can be appreciated. Also worthy of note in this regard are the clubhouses, canteens, and company stores that were created and operated by European corporations in colonial Africa.

Company towns were employed to "modernize" yet another aspect of African culture, namely the concept of family. Traditional African families especially during the European colonial era typically included a man, his multiple wives, and many children. Eurocentric culture and its adherents have always viewed this with disdain. On their part, European colonial authorities and their collaborators actively sought to supplant this aspect of indigenous African tradition with the European equivalent. Thus, it is conceivable that the small rooms that were standard for low-income workers' housing were meant to encourage small family sizes akin to what was obtained in Europe.

6.5 Company Towns That Formed the Nucleus for Large Cities

The implications of company towns for urbanization in Africa are far-reaching. Apart from influencing the lifestyles of their inhabitants and those of surrounding settlements, company towns have formed the nucleus around which major cities have developed on the continent. Examples of these are Kitwe in Zambia, Kaduna in Nigeria, Secunda in South Africa, Tema in Ghana, Mtwara in Tanzania, and Bota/Middle Farms, in Cameroon.

Kitwe, Zambia. Located in the Copperbelt Province of Zambia, Kitwe originated as a company town in 1936. The company town, which formed the nucleus around which the city of Kitwe later expanded, was planned on a modernist model – a model that is typical of European towns. The town was created by the mining conglomerate, Rhodesia Selection Trust (RST) to serve as a hub for its copper mining industry in the region. The discovery of copper deposits in the area around what became the town of Kitwe triggered a rapid influx of miners and the need for infrastructure to accommodate them. The decision by RST to create Kitwe was essentially in response to this need. Thus, Kitwe was created to provide housing, amenities, and services for the mining workforce. As a company town, Kitwe boasted residential units, schools, hospitals, and recreational facilities. These pieces of essential infrastructure led in no small way to the town's rapid growth, especially as more mining operations were established in the surrounding area. Over time, Kitwe grew from the small company town it was in the 1930s into a center not only for mining but also trade, commerce, and services that support other industries apart from copper. Today, it is Zambia's third largest city based on level of infrastructure development and second by population size to Lusaka, the national capital city.

Kaduna, Nigeria. This city was established in 1900 by British colonialists under Lord Lugard, the pioneer colonial governor of Northern Nigeria. At its core was the company town that was created by the Nigerian Railways Corporation to accommodate its employees, offices, and other facilities. For a long time, the town served as a railway hub and administrative center and later evolved to become a major city with a diverse economy, including manufacturing, trade, and services. The city also grew in importance as an administrative center it was designated the capital of colonial Northern Nigeria in 1917. As the railway network expanded and Kaduna became a crucial administrative center, it evolved beyond its initial role as a company town. By establishing and designating Kaduna as a company town, British colonial authorities contributed significantly to the urbanization and economic growth in northern Nigeria. Kaduna remains an important urban center, serving as the capital of Kaduna State and a hub for commerce, industry, and government activities in northern Nigeria.

Secunda, South Africa. This is a planned company town that was built in the 1970s. An entry in the Encyclopedia Britannica describes Secunda as a modern company town in Mpumalanga Province, South Africa (Britannica, 1998). Located 130 kilometers east of Johannesburg, the town was created by Sasol, an integrated energy chemical company, to support its coal-to-liquid and gas-to-liquid plants. Apart from being constructed in the postcolonial era, this company town was part of Sasol's ambitious project to develop synthetic fuel technology using coal and gas resources and to create a dedicated town to accommodate its employees as well as provide it with essential services and infrastructure. The town was meticulously planned along modernist spatial layout lines, and furnished with schools, hospitals, recreational facilities, and other amenities. These are available to members of the company workforce and their families. Not long after it was constructed, the city began to expand beyond the original Sasol facilities, with the presence of other industries and a range of economic activities. Today, Secunda is not only a company town but also a large city in the Gert Sibande District Municipality of Mpumalanga Province in South Africa.

Tema, Ghana. Tema was created as a company town to accommodate employees of Tema Port in Ghana. Work on this port began in 1954, and construction of the meticulously planned company town which occupied the area adjacent to the port, began soon thereafter. The town's development was overseen by the Tema Development Corporation, a Ghanaian parastatal that was created in 1952. This was five years before Ghana gained independence from Britain in 1957. The company town's development was part of the Ghanaian government's deliberate effort to establish a modern port facility and promote industrialization in the country. As part of the efforts to make the town self-contained, authorities ensured the inclusion of residential areas, commercial, and educational institutions, healthcare units, and ancillary facilities. With these facilities, it did not take long for Tema to grow and expand physically and demographically, attracting both domestic and foreign investors. This urbanization process was significantly enhanced by the town's strategic location, particularly its proximity to the national capital city, Accra, and the presence of a deep-water port.

Mtwara, Tanzania. Mtwara was established in the 1970s as a company town by the Tanzania Petroleum Development Corporation to support the petroleum industry in the region. This industry has significantly influenced the town's growth to become a regional center with diverse economic activities. As originally planned, the town included residential areas, offices, schools, hospitals, and cognate amenities, particularly those required for the comfort of employees and their families. It has grown over the years into a large city, thanks to its strategic location near gas fields and access to transportation routes, which make it an ideal base for the petroleum industry. Today, Mtwara is fully urbanized, and a regional center, attracting various industries, businesses, and service providers. In addition to the petroleum industry, the city is engaged in trade, agriculture, fishing, and other economic activities.

Bota/Middle Farms, Cameroon. This company town is one of many that house workers of the Cameroon Development Corporation (CDC), an agro-plantation corporation in Cameroon. The CDC was a conglomerate of private German agricultural firms that came under British colonial control as part of agreements arrived at following the conclusion of World War I. During the German colonial era, and for some time after the British had taken charge and renamed the conglomerate, Commonwealth Development Corporation, workers were responsible for their housing. However, in the 1940s, as called for by some provisions of the British colonial government's Welfare Act of 1940, British colonial authorities in Southern Cameroons moved to develop a series of company towns dedicated to housing the corporation's employees. The Bota/ Middle Farms company town was one of these towns.

The purpose of this carefully planned company town is to provide modern and adequate accommodation for the corporation's workers of all categories. Accordingly, they proceeded to construct modern, European-style housing for laborers, clerical staff, intermediate staff, and senior staff of the corporation. As originally conceived, laborers were provided one-room housing while the clerical staff were assigned two-room units. Both had individual kitchens but shared sanitation facilities. The intermediate staff was provided with one-bedroom self-contained units (including a living room, kitchen, and indoor plumbing). The senior staff, mainly Whites at the time, were provided lavishly furnished three and occasionally four-bedroom bungalows. Each of these was equipped with a bar, a large kitchen, a two-car garage, servants' quarters, a large garden, and an orchard as well as lawns that were maintained by company laborers. Bota/Middle Farms, which also served as the headquarters of CDC, boasted amenities such as a school, a major hospital, and other healthcare units, as well as recreational facilities such as soccer fields, tennis courts, and golf courses. It grew to become a vibrant commercial and industrial hub with economic infrastructure such as a natural deep seaport, a palm oil mill, and an oil refinery. Over time, and especially because of its location on the Atlantic coast, the company town has evolved to become the center from which real estate development has expanded to link up with Limbe (formerly, Victoria) to the east, Isokolo and Ngueme to the west and Mile One and Bonadikombo to the northeast.

6.6 Conclusion

Although often ignored, or only included as a footnote, in discussions of the city in Africa, company towns have contributed in many ways to urbanization on the continent. Usually created by companies in the mining and agricultural sectors to accommodate their workers, these towns were influential in the continent's urbanization process during the colonial era; they remain influential today. Once created, these towns and the economic activities they engender begin to attract a large influx of people in search of work in the mining and agricultural sectors.

Because they are typically located in rural areas, the creation of a company town invariably leads to population growth in a previously rural area. This process is accelerated by the fact that company towns typically include the provisioning of infrastructure such as streets, residential units, schools, hospitals, recreational facilities, and other amenities. The availability of these amenities tends to encourage the emergence of other human settlements in adjacent areas. Company towns throughout Africa have also served as, or been part of, economic hubs in the regions of which they are a part. Through their ability to attract more business and service providers, they have expanded demographically and physically thereby fueling commercial activities, creating employment opportunities, and attracting investment to the area. Apart from the population growth and business opportunities they engender, company towns have always been melting pots comprising people from diverse backgrounds; these people tend to create multicultural and multilingual communities. As a contributing factor to urbanization in Africa, company towns are not exclusively of historical importance. They continue to thrive as the nucleus, and foundation for the growth and development, of cities on the continent.

7 Postcolonial Cities

7.1 Introduction

The 1960s witnessed an important transition in the life of countries in Africa; there was a widespread demise of colonialism on the continent. Since then, African cities have experienced remarkable changes in many areas, particularly concerning urbanization, infrastructure provisioning, commerce, urban and human settlement conditions, and cultural diversity. The seeds of these changes were sowed during the colonial era. For example, urbanization, especially the growth and proliferation of towns and cities were triggered by the rural-to-urban migration trends set in motion by the urban-biased development policies of colonial authorities.

Colonial urban-biased policies resulted in the concentration of pieces of basic public infrastructure in urban areas. Given the shoestring budget of colonial governments, these pieces were paltry, concentrated in the European enclaves and a few privileged urban districts. Consequently, it did not take long into the postcolonial era for the infrastructure to be outpaced by urban demographic and spatial growth. Efforts to develop and add new pieces of infrastructure to the stock inherited from the colonial era have encountered enormous challenges. At the same time, the levels and rates of urbanization have been rapidly increasing. Resulting from this have been a multitude of problems such as the emergence, growth, and proliferation of slums, and informal settlements or shantytowns; these were rare or unknown during the colonial era. Characterized by improvised squalid and dilapidated housing and typically located at the outskirts of cities throughout the continent, these settlements lack the most basic amenities.

However, it would be erroneous to characterize African cities in the post-colony as completely gloomy. They are not! Rather, African cities in the postcolony are vibrant and diverse; they showcase a blend of indigenous and received cultures. Their role as a melting pot for a variety of ethnicities, languages, and religions is unmatched. More importantly, African cities in the postcolony have manifested an impressive degree of versatility in fusing local traditions with global influences; collectively, these have produced unique results in literature, music, and the culinary arts.

Yet, the fact that African cities in the postcolony have unique issues of their own because of their mainly colonial origins is not without ramifications. The most prominent of these relates to the transition from racial to socio-economic spatial segregation. This invokes questions regarding the transfer of exclusively European enclaves to senior members of the postcolonial bureaucracy. Also, of relevance are questions concerning the gated community phenomenon.

7.2 Cities and Metropolises in the Postcolony

Independence had far-reaching implications for the urbanization that was set in motion during the colonial era in Africa. In very few cases, such as Brazzaville and Dakar, which lost their status as federation capitals, the rate of urbanization slowed down, relatively speaking. In other cases, especially those in which new towns – such as Abuja in Nigeria, Dodoma in Tanzania, and Lilongwe in Malawi – were developed the rate accelerated. In addition, the exigencies of postcolonial governance called for the expansion of central administrative facilities, and the creation of subnational or provincial-level administrative centers.

In countries such as South Africa and Kenya, where ostensibly racist policies such as the infamous "pass laws" were in force, the postcolonial era witnessed an influx of Africans into cities to which they were previously denied access. These factors combined to heighten levels of urbanization in colonial and new towns throughout the continent. In making this observation, urban geographer, Bill Freund described how Lagos, Nigeria's capital until 1998, surpassed Ibadan to become the country's most populous city, and by far the most populous in the sub-Saharan region (Freund, 2012). In Zimbabwe, the administrative capital city, Harare (formerly, Salisbury) has surpassed Bulawayo, which used to be the country's industrial center and largest city during the colonial era. In Cameroon, the capital city, Yaounde is fast catching up with Douala, the economic capital thanks to the attention it has received from the political leadership during the postcolonial era.

As was the case during the colonial era, governments remained very powerful; their decisions have continued to rank among the leading determinants of urban growth in the postcolony. The immediate postcolonial era in Africa was marked by an unprecedented expansion of government employment, and before long, the government had become not only the largest employer but by far, the most dominant actor in the formal sector in every African country. In country after country, people from rural areas and other parts of the country flock to the capital in droves with the hopes of gaining employment, especially in the formal sector. Commensurate with this has been the unprecedented growth of the informal sector, especially in cities experiencing significant increases in their public administration roles. This in turn has amplified and accelerated the rural-to-urban migration process, and ultimately the rate and level of urbanization.

The rush by rural peasants to get a piece of whatever action the capital cities offer is not only of academic or policy-making relevance. Rather, it has been a subject at the heart of popular discourse since the immediate postcolonial era. The lyrics of Cameroonian ace folklore musician Talla Andre Marie's song of 1975, "*Je vais à Yaoundé*," paint a lucid picture of the situation. In this song, Talla Andre Marie is singing about the tendency of rural peasants to flock to the cities, particularly the capital city, that was widespread during the immediate postcolonial era in Cameroon. He ponders why a rural peasant would leave the serenity of village life to head to the national capital, Yaounde. Excerpts of the lyrics read thus (Talla, 1975):

> *Où vas-tu paysan avec ton boubou neuf, ton chapeau bariolé, tes souliers écoulés? Ou vas-tu paysan loin de ton village ou tu vivais en paix pres de te caféiers? Je vais à Yaoundé, Yaoundé la capitale.*

> Where are you going peasant with your new boubou, your motley hat, your worn-out shoes? Where are you going peasant far from your village where you lived in peace near your coffee trees? I am going to Yaoundé, Yaoundé the capital.

From the literary arts world, novelists have also chimed in to highlight the deceptive allure of city life in Africa. For example, the Congolese novelist, Mwanza Mujila narrates the story of the mining town of Lubumbashi and how its glittering lights attract rural peasants who sooner or later discover that not all that glitters is not diamond. Focusing on the generic themes of migration, exploitation, and the impact of urbanization on personal identity, the novel vividly captures the experiences of two friends and how they found themselves face-to-face with the dangers of urban life.

Cities, or urban areas writ large continue to be the vehicle through which governments express their ability to keep abreast with global trends in modernization in all domains, including human settlement development, education, health, industrialization, culture, sports, and entertainment. It is therefore hardly any wonder that countries in postcolonial Africa have been in a race to outdo one another concerning grand showcase infrastructure development projects in administrative and/or economic capital cities. As Bill Freund observed, it is in these cities that a new kind of modernity typified by the construction of "such prestige structures as sports stadia and international grade hotels has sprung up on an unprecedented scale" (Freund, 2012: 146). Such projects have been more common in Francophone countries where the administration and governance of cities fall directly under the purview of the national government. In the Ivory Coast, for instance, authorities drew from the country's rich cocoa- and coffee-based economy to construct impressive high-rise structures and office towers in the capital city, Abidjan. Developments of this type that are on the increase in Africa, as Vanessa Watson (2014) once described them, constitute an emerging form of urban fantasies characterized by glass towers and ultra-modern buildings, with associated "dreams" and "nightmares" (Watson, 2014). To these, Bandauko and colleagues have added the emergence of a new phenomenon in African cities, namely

"American-style shopping malls, wealthy Western-style gated communities, new financial and commercial districts, mega urban infrastructure such as highways and flyovers ... . and planned smart eco-cities such as Eko Atlantic City, Lagos" (Bandauko et al., 2022: 339).

7.3 From Racial to Socio-Economic Spatial Segregation

If the colonial city in Africa was characterized by racial segregation, the African city in the postcolony is known for its socio-economic compartmentalization schemes. This came about by a simple means. Upon the demise of colonialism, the indigenous leadership moved swiftly to take over and transfer to senior members of the emerging independent government exclusive European enclaves of the colonial era. Similarly, the areas that served as the living quarters of intermediate-level members of the colonial public service were assigned to functionaries of equivalent levels in the emerging public bureaucracy. For example, in Buea, which served as the capital of German Kamerun, the senior functionaries of the independent government inherited the colonial era exclusive European enclave at the Government Reservation Area (GRA) Bokwango, while the midlevel government employees inherited the Clerks' Quarters across from Great Soppo and uphill from Small Soppo. Thus, the landscape that used to be segregated by race has become compartmentalized according to socio-economic class.

In colonial British northern Nigeria, particularly in the ancient city of Kano, there was, according to Albert (1994), a successful effort to reorder built space. In this case, British colonial administrators had divided the city into three segregated districts, including Birni, Sabon Gari, and the Township. Birni was occupied exclusively by the precolonial Hausa/Fulani Kanawa. Immigrants from other parts of Nigeria and Africa were settled in Sabon Gari, including Tundum-Wada and Gwargwarma. The Township was an exclusive European enclave. Once Nigeria gained independence, this enclave was transferred to top civil servants, public establishments, and major companies in Kano (Albert, 1994).

The postcolonial era witnessed four new, or previously little-known, developments in the urban landscape in Africa. In no order, these include the emergence or expansion of, gated communities, strangers' quarters, new cities or new towns, and slum settlements. Gated communities, which are residential facilities enclosed by walls or fences, and manned- or electronic security-monitored gates, have become increasingly commonplace in major cities in Africa. Similarly, new cities bear a striking resemblance to gated communities but differ because they are usually master-planned and often detached from extant cities. Table 2 shows a sample of gated communities and what they have to offer.

Both new cities and gated communities in general tend to exacerbate problems of social-spatial segregation and socio-economic differentials. Also, they perpetuate socio-economic inequalities and contribute to urban fragmentation. Through their ability to create physical and social barriers, they can limit interaction and reinforce segregation between different socio-economic groups within cities. By their very definition as enclosed or fenced residential communities, they are automatically exclusionary; only people with the financial wherewithal can afford to live in them. Their tendency to be exclusive is their *raison d'être* as they are often advertised as a viable strategy for protecting oneself and property from criminals. Additionally, such communities have been promoted as a means of showcasing occupants' wealth and ability to keep abreast with global trends. African cities in the postcolonial era have always been in a race to attain a goal – the goal of looking like cities in the West – that appears to be an ever-receding mirage. Why is this the case? The following assertion by Lesley Lokko in the *City Monitor* hints at the response to this perennial question. "Like it or not, we measure the success – or failure – of cities according to broad principles of urban culture inherited largely from the West" (Lokko, 2017).

Societal elites, particularly members of the higher socio-economic strata in African cities, are doing exactly what Europeans did during the colonial era; they have monopolized access to necessary urban goods and services. Paradoxical situations such as this could be what Fassil Demissie (2008) had in mind when he opined that the city in Africa today is caught in the contradiction of an imperial past and a postcolonial present. Traces of Africa's colonial past continue to reverberate in cities throughout the continent more than half a century since the widespread demise of colonialism. Foremost in this regard are the stranger quarters and slum settlements that emerged in large towns when people immigrated from distant locations to take advantage of the economic opportunities resulting from colonial initiatives.

7.4 Stranger Quarters

Defined as areas containing persons who are nonindigenous to the town or city in which they live, contemporary stranger quarters in Africa have their roots in the colonial era. Prominent among Africa's stranger quarters are Yeoville, Johannesburg in South Africa, Little Mogadishu (or Eastleigh), Nairobi in Kenya, Medina, Dakar in Senegal, Kariakoo, Dar es Salaam in Tanzania, Sabon Gari, Kano in Nigeria, and New Bell, Douala in Cameroon.

Yeoville, South Africa. Yeoville was created as a suburb of Johannesburg in 1890; this was barely four years after the discovery of gold that inspired the establishment of Johannesburg. In its early days, the area was promoted as a "sanitarium for wealthy persons"; thanks to its elevation, the air in Yeoville was purer than the dirty, smoke-filled mining town that evolved from the Transvaal bushveld. However, contrary to the hopes of its creators, Yeoville ended up attracting not the rich but migrants of different socio-economic strata mainly from outside South Africa. Yeoville has a very rich history, including the fact that it once provided refuge to South Africa's first indigenous African president, Nelson Mandela. This is when he was on the run from the police in the early 1960s. The place has always been on an upward swing since its creation. However, as of the 1990s, it began experiencing a steady decline that accelerated in the mid 1990s when its management began going into disarray. This was compounded by the fact that it experienced a demographic transition, particularly, "white flight," as it changed from an 85-percent White to a 90-percent Black community in 1998. Since the 2000s, Yeoville has firmly established itself as a cultural melting pot comprising economic migrants from other parts of South Africa and Africa at large.

Little Mogadishu (or Eastleigh). This is a neighborhood in Nairobi, Kenya. It is home to a significant Somali community. As a neighborhood dominated by non-Kenyans, that is, a "stranger quarters," Little Mogadishu is different from most stranger neighborhoods in Africa because its roots are not traceable to the colonial era. Rather, the neighborhood was established in the 1990s as a refuge for some victims of the civil war in Somalia. Most of the victims who escaped to

Table 2 Prominent gated communities in Africa

Item	Name of community	City	Country	Remarks
01.	Eko Atlantic City	Lagos	Nigeria	This facility promotes itself as secure and luxurious living environment with modern infrastructure, waterfront views, and upscale amenities.
02.	Waterfall Estate	Johannesburg	South Africa	This facility contains different housing options, including apartments, townhouses, and bungalows. In addition, it advertises itself as providing extensive security measures, green spaces, recreational facilities and commercial areas.
03.	Runda Estate	Nairobi	Kenya	It advertises itself as containing luxurious homes, landscaped gardens, and 24-hour security.
04.	Le Jardin de Fleur	Marrakech	Morocco	It promotes itself as offering privacy and security, with amenities such as swimming pools, tennis courts, and a clubhouse.
05.	Zamalek, Egypt	Cairo	Egypt	This advertises itself as offering a mix of apartments and villas, and private gardens and recreational facilities as well as a sense of exclusivity.

Source: Author's compilation.

Kenya congregated in Eastleigh, a neighborhood in Kenya's capital city, Nairobi. Before long, the neighborhood had become mostly comprised of Somali refugees and nicknamed Little Mogadishu after Somalia's capital city, Mogadishu. Gradually, it evolved into a veritably vibrant community – a home away from home for Somalians in Nairobi. A significant number of the early Somali settlers indulged in different activities and went into commercial businesses of all sorts. Today, the neighborhood is a bustling economic hub not only for Nairobi-based Somali refugees but also for economic migrants and businesspeople from other parts of East and Southern Africa. It is essentially a global hub for Somali and other businesses.

However, the community's residents, writes Neil Carrier, are often held under suspicion because they are believed to be linked to Islamic terrorism (Carrier, 2016). This suspicion appears to have been reinforced following the 2013 Westgate Mall attack for which some Islamic groups claimed responsibility. Some of the residents are also alleged to be involved in illegal activities, not least of which are counterfeiting and piracy. One way by which the Kenyan government has sought to deal with the neighborhood's security and crime problem is to invest in urban development projects. These have included projects to improve streets, sanitation, and social services. Currently, the neighborhood constitutes a testament to the resilience, entrepreneurship, and cultural vibrancy of the Nairobi-based Somali community. More importantly, it has contributed enormously to the cosmopolitan tapestry of Kenya's capital city, Nairobi.

Medina, Dakar in Senegal. Medina, a predominantly strangers' neighborhood in Dakar, traces its roots to the colonial era in Senegal. It was established to accommodate Dakar's growing population during the heydays of the French colonial era in the 19th century. The nucleus of the neighborhood is its bustling market, the Medina Market or *Marchê Medina* (in French), which is one of the largest and busiest in all of Senegal. Yet, the market is not the only fixture deserving of attention in Medina; rather, there is a subdistrict known as Medina Gounass that cannot go unnoticed even by the passive observer. It is especially important to the Mouride Brotherhood, a leading Sufi Islamic order. Medina Gounass serves as the venue for this order's annual religious festival, "Gamou," which attracts thousands of pilgrims from Senegal and other parts of the world. The neighborhood's religious identity is hard to miss as it is home to the Grand Mosque of Dakar or the Mosque of Divinity. This is an iconic landmark, which serves as a major place of worship for the Muslims in Dakar. Culturally, Medina is markedly cosmopolitan as it contains a mix of ethnic groups, including Wolof, Serer, Toucouleur, and Lebanese. Mirroring this diversity are the neighborhood's architecture, cuisine, music, and art in general. In this latter regard, Medina has been a major player on the Senegalese music scene; in fact, the neighborhood has made a significant contribution to Mbalax, a popular form of music in the region. Concerning urban planning, municipal authorities in Dakar often find themselves wrestling with the question of how to go about modernizing the neighborhood while retaining its distinct character and traditional charm. Nevertheless, they have succeeded in the recent past in improving its infrastructure, including the roads, utilities, and public spaces. Today, Medina is a lively neighborhood that embodies Dakar's cultural tapestry and history; it contains not only its namesake market but also major religious landmarks as well as artistic artifacts that contribute to the region's vibrancy and dynamism.

Sabon Gari, Kano in Nigeria. This is one of the best-known strangers' quarters in Africa. Located in Kano, one of Africa's cities with roots in antiquity, Sabon Gari was established during Nigeria's colonial era. It began as a new town – or *sabon gari*, in Hausa – for nonindigenous inhabitants, particularly Europeans, Lebanese, and immigrants from other parts of Nigeria and Africa as a whole. Areas reserved for nonindigenous persons are particularly commonplace in large Nigerian towns. Writing in *Refworld*, an online publication, the Immigration and Refugee Board of Canada (IRBC), observed that every large town in southern Nigeria has a Hausa community (or a Hausa Quarters), clustered around a mosque, just as every big town in northern Nigeria boasts a Sabon Gari (or a Strangers' Quarters) (IRBC, 2002).

As noted earlier, the British colonial authorities in Nigeria had created Sabon Gari, Kano, as a segregated space to separate immigrants from the indigenous Hausa and Muslim inhabitants of Kano. Each group contributes to the community's socio-cultural fabric and political economy. The Igbos, Lebanese, and Indians dominate the area's entrepreneurial class, commercial, and manufacturing sectors. They make Sabon Gari, and in fact, Kano in general an important commercial hub in West Africa. It is well-known for its wide range of goods, including textiles, apparel, electronic goods, household items, food, and hide. Sabon Gari also boasts one of the most vibrant informal sectors in Nigeria and West Africa as a whole with numerous participants in the cottage industrial and artisanal sectors, hawking, and street vending.

Sabon Gari's multiethnic and multicultural composition has boded both well and ill for its livelihood. The major riots that the area has experienced during Nigeria's colonial and postcolonial eras have their roots in this aspect of its makeup. The ancient city of Kano of which Sabon Gari is a part has been a hotbed of violent conflicts during the colonial and postcolonial eras. Most of these have either started or been intensified, in Sabon Gari. One such riot is notable especially because it claimed at least seventy lives. It occurred in late July 1999 and involved mainly members of the Yoruba ethnic group from southern Nigeria and Hausa people from northern Nigeria. The riot is also noteworthy because it is generally understood to have been rooted in long-standing and simmering animosity between the mainly Christian southerners and predominantly Muslim northerners of Nigeria.

Kariakoo, Dar es Salaam in Tanzania. This settlement began as a small trading post in the late 19th century. Its name, "Karia-Koo," is Swahili for "small or little village." The Indian community in Dar es Salaam has historically influenced the growth and development of the neighborhood. Not only is Kariakoo a pre-independence fixture on the landscape of Dar es Salaam, but it also played a major role in Tanzania's struggle for independence from British colonial rule. In this connection, it served as a center for political activism, with its residents actively participating in anti-colonial protests and demonstrations.

Kariakoo has always been a commercial hub with persons of Indian extraction always counting among its main traders and merchants while indigenous Africans from the hinterland and other parts of Tanzania have historically dominated its small-scale business and informal sector ranks. Today, the Kariakoo market stands as one of Dar es Salaam's largest and most vibrant markets, drawing traders and customers of assorted goods from all over Tanzania, eastern and southern Africa, and the Middle East. Collectively, the entrepreneurs, traders, and street vendors operating in Kariakoo contribute to its local economy as they generate employment opportunities. As those who patronize the market, the inhabitants of Kariakoo are also diverse; they are persons of Swahili, Arab, Indian, and indigenous African extraction. Thanks, at least partially, to its diversity and the multicultural make-up of its inhabitants, the neighborhood has become a venue for cultural events that draw participants from different ethnicities and parts of the world.

7.5 Slum and Squatter Settlements

By the time of the widespread decolonization process in Africa in the 1960s, urban populations had significantly increased. However, there was no corresponding surge in the quantity of public infrastructure, housing, and related services. Rather, there was an unprecedented growth in the volume of substandard and overcrowded housing that lacked basic amenities – in other words, slums and/or squatter settlements – in urban areas throughout the continent. The proliferation of slum and squatter settlements was also fueled by the lifting of the laws and other pieces of legislation that restricted the access of Africans to urban areas. In countries that had experienced prolonged civil wars, such as Liberia, Sierra Leone, Angola, and Mozambique, the prevalence of slum and squatter settlements often resulted from many people being forced to the city to escape war-ravaged conditions in the rural areas. As Barros and Balsas (2019) observed in the case of Angola, the capital city, Luanda, which had a population of half a million at the end of the Portuguese colonial era in 1975, now has more than 10 million persons. As many as 7 million (70 percent) of these live in informal slum settlements; in the case of Luanda, the capital, the slums are paradoxically located in the central parts of the city. Thus, slum and squatter settlements emerged, grew, and proliferated to accommodate the ever-increasing populations that have been migrating from rural areas in search of better economic opportunities in towns and cities throughout the continent.

Often made up of makeshift components such as scrapped corrugated and other metal, cardboards, and pieces of discarded industrial crates, the typically owner-constructed units comprising squatter settlements are usually created on vacant unused land without legal permission or property rights. Such settlements usually have very limited access to basic utility and healthcare facilities. Unemployment and lack of educational facilities as well as the absence of property rights and insecure land tenure conspire to further create difficulties for the residents who are often vulnerable to eviction and displacement.

Access to land is an important but oft-ignored determinant of the incidence of squatter settlements. The research of Margaret Peil in the 1970s was very enlightening in this regard. She considered it paradoxical that while poverty levels and rate of rural-to-urban exodus were as high in West Africa as in East and Southern Africa during the immediate postcolonial era, West Africa was almost devoid of the problem of squatter settlements. This paradox, Peil explained, was because in West Africa, family-based and cognate social ties often obligate people to assist one another. Such assistance usually includes but is not limited to providing accommodation to new rural immigrants in urban areas. Also, in West Africa, in contrast to elsewhere, rural immigrants in towns and cities always harbor the notion of returning to their rural areas of origin. Hence, they are comfortable with the idea of renting housing. Finally, the cost of land, as Peil noted, is also more affordable in the West than in East Africa.

The story of slums and squatter settlements in Africa is incomplete without mention of Kibera, which is reputed as the continent's largest slum, and the series of slums in Luanda in Angola, which defy the norm by their location at the center as opposed to the outskirts of the city. Covering an area of about 2.5 square kilometers (about 1 square mile) and containing a population in the hundreds of thousands, Kiberia is considered Africa's largest slum and squatter settlement. It was created in the 20th century as a temporary settlement for Nubian soldiers who had fought for the British colonial forces in World War I. With time, it attracted poor people from different parts of the country hoping to find better economic opportunities in the capital city, Nairobi.

The most prominent of Luanda's slums include Sambizanga, Mota, and Marcal, which emerged during the colonial era in Angola. They are a by-product of the colonial government's racial segregation and European-biased development policies. These policies neglected African neighborhoods by directing most urban development initiatives exclusively to exclusively European enclaves. When the country became independent in 1975, the European enclaves were inherited by senior members of the country's bureaucracy. These enclaves have since continued to be the exclusive targets of urban development initiatives. Essentially, the racially segregated population of the colonial era has become a wealth-segregated population. At the same time, the urban population continues to rapidly grow, and so do the slum settlements.

7.6 Conclusion

Postcolonial African cities differ from their precolonial and colonial predecessors in many ways. Postcolonial cities, a few of which evolved from ancient times through the colonial period, have undergone many significant changes. For one thing, postcolonial cities are experiencing a rate of urbanization that could only have been imagined during the precolonial and colonial eras. Also, postcolonial cities are physically larger and boast significantly larger populations than their predecessors. This growth has been fueled by a variety of factors, not least of which is more rapid rural-to-urban migration. Finally, precolonial cities were generally smaller and more localized, serving as political and economic hubs for the surrounding regions. For another thing, precolonial and colonial era cities were more orderly than their postcolonial counterparts. During the colonial era, cities, especially capital cities, in Africa were generally planned and developed as a component of the colonial project. At the same time, colonial urban planning sought to create racially segregated urban spaces, with exclusive European enclaves, and compartmentalized land uses. In contrast, postcolonial cities have transformed racially segregated, into socio-economically segregated, spaces.

References

Abydos, W. M. F. (2023). Gold, Salt, and Islam: The Story of Koumbi Saleh | Ancient Origins (ancient-origins.net). Abydos | World Monuments Fund (wmf.org).

Albert, I. O. (1994). Violence in metropolitan Kano: A historical perspective. In *Urban Violence in Africa: Pilot Studies (South Africa, Côte-d'Ivoire, Nigeria)* (pp. 111–136). IFRA-Nigeria. https://doi.org/10.4000/books.ifra.788.

Andrews, E. (2017). 7 Influential African Empires. Available online at History: A&E Television Network. Accessed, May 17, 2023 via: www.history.com/news/7-influential-african-empires (Originally published: January 11, 2017).

Bandauko, E., Arku, G., & Nyantakyi-Frimpong, H. (2022). A systematic review of gated communities and the challenge of urban transformation in African cities. *Journal of Housing and the Built Environment*, 37: 339–368. https://doi.org/10.1007/s10901-021-09840-1.

Barros, C. P. & Balsas, C. J. L. (2019). Luanda's slums: An overview based on poverty and gentrification. *Urban Development Issues*, 64: 29–38. https://doi.org/10.2478/udi-2019-0021.

Berman, B. J. (2010). *Ethnicity and Democracy in Africa*. Tokyo: JICA Research Institute.

Britannica (2024). Karmah Archaeological Site, Sudan. Accessed, March 17, 2024 via: www.britannica.com/place/Karmah.

Britannica, T. Editors of Encyclopaedia (1998, July 20). Secunda. Encyclopedia Britannica. Accessed, July 4, 2023 via: www.britannica.com/place/Secunda.

Carrier, N. (2016). *Little Mogadishu: Eastleigh, Nairobi's global Somali hub.* Oxford: Oxford University Press.

Chikowero, M. (2007). Subalternating currents: Electrification and power politics in Bulawayo, colonial Zimbabwe, 1894–1939. *Journal of Southern African Studies*, 33(2): 287–306. www.jstor.org/stable/25065197.

Cloete, J. & Marais, L. (2019). Mine housing in the South African coalfields: The unforeseen consequences of post-apartheid policy. *Housing Studies*, 36(9): 1388–1406.

Coquery-Vidrovitch, C. (2009). *The History of African Cities South of the Sahara: From Origins to Colonization*. Princeton, NJ: Markus Wiener.

Cottrell, L. (1957). *Lost Cities*. New York: Holt, Rinehart and Winston.

Demissie, F. (ed.) (2008). *Postcolonial African Cities: Imperial Legacies and Postcolonial Predicament*. London: Routledge.

Dennis, P. (2006). A Brief History of Liberia. Accessed, June 8, 2023 via The International Centre for Justice. PeacebuildingData.org. www.ictj.org/publi cation/brief-history-liberia.

Ducksters (2023). Ancient Egypt Cities. Online publication by ducsters.com. Accessed, May 22, 2023 via: www.ducksters.com/history/ancient_egypt/ cities_of_ancient_egypt.php.

Encyclopedia Almanacs (2023). Cape Colony and Cape Town. Accessed, July 7, 2023 via: www.encyclopedia.com/history/encyclopedias-almanacs-transcripts-and-maps/cape-colony-and-cape-town

Encyclopedia Britannica (2023). Djenne-Djenno: Ancient City of Mali. Accessed, July 7, 2023 via: www.britannica.com/place/Djenne-Jeno

Encyclopedia.com (2023). Colonial Cities and Towns, Africa. Accessed, March 9, 2023 via: www.encyclopedia.com/history/encyclopedias-almanacs-transcripts-and-maps/colonial-cities-and-towns-africa#:~:text=Such%20towns%20as% 20Accra%20(Ghana,administrative%20centers%20of%20imperialist% 20expansion.

Freund, B. (2012). *The African City: A History.* Cambridge: Cambridge University Press. https://doi.org/10.1017/CBO9780511618307.

Geography (2023). West African Trading Settlements. Accessed, June 6, 2023 via: https://geography.name/west-african-trading-settlements/.

GPN (2023). Castles and Forts. Accessed, June 9, 2023 via Ghana Place Names (GPN). At: https://sites.google.com/site/ghanaplacenames/places-in-perspec tive/castles-forts.

Hall, P. (1962). *The World Cities.* New York: McGraw-Hill.

Hall, P. (1966). *The World Cities.* London: World University Library, Weidenfeld & Nicolson.

Hatshetpsut (2024). Koumbi Saleh: The Ancient Capital of Ghana. Positive African History. Accessed, March 16, 2024 via: www.hatshepsut.co/koumbi-saleh/.

Hay, A. & Harris, R. (2007). 'Shauri ya Sera Kali': The colonial regime of urban housing in Kenya to 1939. *Urban History,* 34(3): 504–530. https://doi.org/ 10.1017/S096392680700497X [ALISON HAY and RICHARD HARRIS].

History (2023). 7 Influential African Empires. Online publication. Accessed, May 17, 2023 via: www.history.com/news/7-influential-african-empires.

Home, R. K. (1997). *Of Planting and Planning: The Making of British Colonial Cities.* London: E & FN Spon.

Home, R. K. (2000). From barrack compounds to the single-family house: Planning worker housing in Colonial Natal and Northern Rhodesia. *Planning Perspectives,* 15: 327–347.

Hull, R. W. (1976). *African Cities and Towns before the European Conquest.* London: W.W. Norton.

Hunt, P.N. (2017). *Hannibal.* New York: Simon & Schuster.

IRBC (2002). *Nigeria: Riots in Sabon Gari in 1999,* (Immigration and Refugee Board of Canada, December 12, 2002), NGA40452.EF. Accessed, June 23, 2023 via: www.refworld.org/docid/3f7d4de27.html.

Khan Academy (2024). African Societies and the Beginning of the Atlantic Slave Trade. Accessed, March 13, 2024 via: www.khanacademy.org/human ities/us-history/precontact-and-early-colonial-era/before-contact/a/african-societies-and-the-beginning-of-the-atlantic-slave-trade.

Koutinin, M. (2016). Story of Cities #5: Benin City, The Mighty Medieval Capital now Lost Without Trace. An online article in The Guardian.com. Accessed, June 10, 2023 via: www.theguardian.com/cities/2016/mar/18/ story-of-cities-5-benin-city-edo-nigeria-mighty-medieval-capital-lost-without-trace#:~:text=Indeed%2C%20they%20classified%20Benin%20City,as %20the%20eye%20can%20see.

Law, R. (1991). *The Slave Coast of West Africa, 1550–1750: The Impact of the Atlantic Slave Trade on an African Society.* Oxford: Oxford University Press.

Lewis, D. (2014). *Monrovia, Liberia (1822 –).* BlackPast.org. www.blackpast .org/global-african-history/places-global-african-history/monrovia-liberia-1821/.

Lokko, L. (2017). Johannesburg and Accra: Two very different versions of a contemporary African city. *City Monitor.* (July6, 2017 updated 19 Jul 2021). Accessed, June 30, 2023 via: https://citymonitor.ai/community/johannesburg-and-accra-two-very-different-versions-contemporary-african-city-2983.

Mabin, A., (1993). Capital, coal and conflict: The genesis of planning a company town in Indwe. *Contree,* 34: 21–31.

Mark, J. J. (2016, February 24). *Thebes (Egypt). World History Encyclopedia.* Retrieved from www.worldhistory.org/Thebes_(Egypt)/.

Mazrui, A. (1986). *The Africans: A Triple Heritage.* Boston,MA: Little Brown.

Modelski, G. (1997). Cities of the Ancient World: An Inventory (-3500 to -1200). Accessed, May 17, 2023 via: https://web.archive.org/web/20140519232105/ https://faculty.washington.edu/modelski/WCITI2.html.

Morris, J. (1963). *Cities: Contemporary History Reflected in Views of Seventy-Four Cities Around the World.* New York: Harcourt, Brace, & World.

National Geographic (2023). Mansa Musa (Musa I of Mali). Online article accessed, May 29, 2023 via: Mansa Musa (Musa I of Mali) (nationalgeo-graphic.org).

Njoh, A. J. (1999). *Urban Planning, Housing and Spatial Structures in Sub-Saharan Africa: Nature, Impact and Development Implications of Exogenous Forces*. Aldershot: Ashgate.

Njoh, A. J. (2006). *Tradition, Culture and Development in Africa: Historical Lessons for Modern Development Planning*. Aldershot: Ashgate.

Njoh, A. J. (2007). *Planning Power: Town Planning and Social Control in Africa*. London: University College London (UCL) Press.

Njoh, A. J. (2008). Colonial philosophies, urban space, and racial segregation in British and French colonial Africa. *Journal of Black Studies*, 38(4): 579–599. https://doi.org/10.1177/0021934706288447.

Njoh, A. J. (2010). Europeans, modern urban planning and the acculturation of "racial others." *Planning Theory*, 9(4): 369–378. https://doi.org/10.1177/1473095210368880. http://plt.sagepub.com.

Njoh, A.J. (2016). *French Urbanism in Foreign Lands*. Cham, Switzerland: Springer.

Njoh, A. J. (2022), French ecological imperialism: A postcolonial approach. *American Journal of Economics and Sociology*, 81: 581–619. https://doi.org/10.1111/ajes.12477

Njoh, A. J. & Bigon, L. (2015). Germany and the deployment of urban planning to create, reinforce and maintain power in colonial Cameroon. *Habitat International*, 49: 10–20.

Njoh, A. J., Chie, E. P., & Bigon, L. (2020). CDC company towns in Cameroon: A case of shaping built space to articulate power and social control in colonial and postcolonial perspectives. *Journal of West African History*, 6(1): 91–112. https://doi.org/10.14321/jwestafrihist.6.1.0091.

Noorloos, van F. (*2018*). *Africa's New Cities: The Contested Future of Urbanisation*. www.researchgate.net/publication/318660587_Africa%27s_new_cities_The_contested_future_of_urbanisation [accessed Jun 19, 2023].

Pearce, F. (1992). The African Queen. Accessed, June 10, 2023 via: www.newscientist.com/article/mg16322035-100-the-african-queen/.

Porteus, J.D. (1970). The nature of the company town. *Transactions of the Institute British Geographers*, 51: 127–42.

Prussin, L. (1986). *Hatumere: Islamic Design in West Africa*. Los Angeles, CA: University of California Press.

Reimer, M. J., Rowlatt, M., & Mackie, J. A. (2023). Alexandria. Entry in the Encyclopedia Britannica. Accessed, May 23, 2023 via: www.britannica.com/place/Alexandria-Egypt.

Sattertwaite, D. (2021). African Cities from 500 AD to 1900. African-cities.org. Accessed, March 9, 2023 via: www.african-cities.org/african-cities-from-500-ad-to-1900/.

Snowden, F. (1991). *Before Color Prejudice: The Ancient View of Blacks.* Cambridge, MA: Harvard University Press.

Silverberg, R. (1962). *Lost Cities and Vanished Civilizations.* Philadelphia, PA/ New York: Chilton Company.

Sittert, L. V. (2001). 'Velddrift': The making of a South African company town. *Urban History*, 28(2): 194–217. www.jstor.org/stable/44613235.

Talla, A.-M. (1975). Je vais è Yaounde, la capitale. Accessed, May 9, 2023 via: www.youtube.com/watch?v=K0Y4yMJeNMw.

Tordoff, W. (1984). *Government and Politics in Africa.* London: Macmillan.

UNESCO (2023). Mbanza Kongo, Vestiges of the Capital of the former Kingdom of Kongo. UNESCO World Heritage Centre. Accessed, May 31, 2023 via: Mbanza Kongo, Vestiges of the Capital of the former Kingdom of Kongo – UNESCO World Heritage Centre.

Watson, V. (2014). African urban fantasies: Dreams or nightmares? *Environment and Urbanization*, 26(1): 215–231.

Watt, van der P. & Marais, L. (2019). Normalising mining company towns in Emalahleni, South Africa. *The Extractive Industries and Society*, 6(4): 1205–1214.

Whatley, W. C. (2014). The transatlantic slave trade and the evolution of political authority in West Africa. In E. Akyeampong, R. H. Bates, N. Nunn, & J. Robinson (Eds.), *Africa's Development in Historical Perspective* (pp. 460–488). Cambridge: Cambridge University Press.

WHE (2023). Memphis (Ancient Egypt). Online Publication by World History Encyclopedia (WHE). Accessed, May 23, 2023 via: www.worldhistory.org/ Memphis_%28Ancient_Egypt%29/.

Wikipedia (2024). Ghana Empire. Accessed, March 16, 2024 via: https://en .wikipedia.org/wiki/Ghana_Empire.

Wikimedia Commons (2023). Photo Gallery of Wikimedia Commons. Available free of charge to the public. Retrieved, May 9, 2023 from: https:// commons.wikimedia.org/wiki/File:Gondar_Castle_40_(27886071584).jpg.

Winters, C. (1982). Urban Morphogenesis in Francophone Black Africa. Geographical Review, 72(2): 139–54.

Wirth, L. (1938). Urbanism as a way of life. *The American Journal of Sociology*, 44(1): 1–24

WMC (2023). Memphis. Retrieved from Wikimedia Commons (WMC). Retrieved, May 23, 2023 at: https://commons.wikimedia.org/wiki/File:Memphis200401 .JPG).

World Atlas (2023). 8 Largest Cities of Ancient Egypt. Online publication accessed May 22, 2023. via: www.worldatlas.com/ancient-world/8-largest-cities-of-ancient-egypt.html.

World History (2021). Elephantine: 9 Things That You Need To Know About The Ancient Egyptian City. Accessed, May 25, 2023 via: Elephantine: 9 Things That You Need To Know About The Ancient Egyptian City – World History Edu.

Cambridge Elements ☰

Global Urban History

Michael Goebel

Graduate Institute Geneva

Michael Goebel is the Pierre du Bois Chair Europe and the World and Associate Professor of International History at the Graduate Institute Geneva. His research focuses on the histories of nationalism, of cities, and of migration. He is the author of *Anti-Imperial Metropolis: Interwar Paris and the Seeds of Third World Nationalism* (2015).

Tracy Neumann

Wayne State University

Tracy Neumann is an Associate Professor of History at Wayne State University. Her research focuses on global and transnational approaches to cities and the built environment. She is the author of *Remaking the Rust Belt: The Postindustrial Transformation of North America* (2016) and of essays on urban history and public policy.

Joseph Ben Prestel

Freie Universität Berlin

Joseph Ben Prestel is an Assistant Professor (wissenschaftlicher Mitarbeiter) of history at Freie Universität Berlin. His research focuses on the histories of Europe and the Middle East in the nineteenth and twentieth centuries as well as on global and urban history. He is the author of *Emotional Cities: Debates on Urban Change in Berlin and Cairo, 1860–1910* (2017).

About the Series

This series proposes a new understanding of urban history by reinterpreting the history of the world's cities. While urban history has tended to produce single-city case studies, global history has mostly been concerned with the interconnectedness of the world. Combining these two approaches produces a new framework to think about the urban past. The individual titles in the series emphasize global, comparative, and transnational approaches. They deliver empirical research about specific cities, while also exploring questions that expand the narrative outside the immediate locale to give insights into global trends and conceptual debates. Authored by established and emerging scholars whose work represents the most exciting new directions in urban history, this series makes pioneering research accessible to specialists and non-specialists alike.

Cambridge Elements $\equiv$

Global Urban History

Printed in the United States
by Baker & Taylor Publisher Services